Also available in the Classmates series:

Teaching Poetry

Fred Sedgwick

continuum
LONDON • NEW YORK

Continuum

The Tower Building
11 York Road
London SE1 7NX
www.continuumbooks.com

15 East 26th Street
New York
NY 10010

First published 2003

British Library Cataloguing-in-Publication Data
A catalogue record for this book is available from the British Library.

ISBN 0-8264-6423-8

Typeset by Originator Publishing Services, Gt Yarmouth
Printed in Great Britain by Biddles Ltd, Guildford and King's Lynn

Contents

Series Introduction

Dear Teacher

Classmates is an exciting and innovative new series developed by Continuum, and is designed to help you improve your teaching and your career.

With your huge workload, both inside and outside of school, we understand that you have less time to read around your profession. These short, pithy guides have been designed with an accessible layout so that you do not have to wade through lots of dull, heavy text to find the information you need.

All of our authors have first-hand teaching experience and have written this essential series with busy teachers in mind. Our subjects range from taking school trips (*Tips for Trips*) and dealing with parents (*Involving Parents*) to coping with the large amounts of stress in your life (*Stress Busting*) and creating more personal time for yourself (*Every Minute Counts*).

If you have practical advice that you would like to share with your fellow teachers and think that you could write a book for this series, then we would be delighted to hear from you.

We do hope that you enjoy reading our Classmates. With very best wishes

Continuum's Education Team

P.S. Watch out for our second batch of ten Classmates, to be launched in March 2004

i.m. FRS (1909–1975)

A candle in Durham, east
of 'the relicts of St Cuthbert';

a candle in St Albans
near 'the relicts of the martyr';

coins in cathedral England –
Canterbury, Chichester, Peterborough –

dropped into wax-encrusted boxes,
made holy, I can only hope, with valid silences ...

Prayers sent into the unknown
for you, my unbelieving father.

Acknowledgements

The following primary schools:

Suffolk: Gislingham and Middleton
Hertfordshire: Hartsfield and Baldock
Durham: Deaf Hill and Montalbo
Norfolk: Tacolneston
Cambridgeshire: St Albans RC VPA

The Education Action Zone in Thetford, Norfolk

The following individuals: Dawn Sedgwick, Henry Burns Eliot, Emily Roeves, Julie Westrop and Linda Skepelhorn.

Introduction

'Hey nonny no and bloody daffodils'

You can, without too much simplification, divide the history of poetry teaching in primary schools over the last 50 years into two periods. This division is applicable for the history of many other things: popular music, attitudes to sex, the standing of young people (I am thinking here of the invention of the teenager). Before 1963, 'Between', as Philip Larkin (1988) famously wrote, 'the end of the *Chatterley* ban / And the Beatles' first LP', nearly all books on teaching poetry described children doing one or more of four things. First, they learned it by heart or by rote. There is an important distinction in these terms which is embedded in the very words: are feelings involved, or is the learning a matter of 'mechanical practice, routine, exercise of memory without proper understanding' (SOED, 1973).

Second, the children recited poetry. Many readers over the age of 50 will remember the stress involved in standing up in front of the class or, worse, an audience of parents, and reciting prepared poems that usually had nothing to do with their ordinary lives. There was also 'choral speaking', when poems were spoken in unison. This seems to be now a contradiction of part (at least since the romantic age) of the essence

1

of poetry: its insistence on the primary of the individual and his or her imagination.

Third, the children listened to poetry. The words 'Now, children, we are going to have some poetry', usually meant 'Now children, we are going to take a break from reality, and the way I speak will suit the ethereal nature of the subject matter of these poems . . . '.

Fourth, the children 'appreciated' poetry. I can recall this best by thinking of the 'music appreciation' classes in my grammar school, circa 1958: Sir plays a record of the *Hebrides Overture* by Mendelssohn, and we boys listen to it. 'Can you hear the sound of the waves on the rocks?' Similarly, we had to 'appreciate' 'great' poetry: Shakespeare, of course, usually in patriotic mood, with the speech before Harfleur from *Henry V*, and Thomas Gray ('Elegy in a Country Churchyard') among others.

There was no writing involved in 'poetry appreciation'. Because my books, so far, have extensively discussed children writing poetry, it might be assumed that I feel that my post-sixties generation of teachers, who were concerned with children writing rather than appreciating poetry, got it right. I certainly did feel that, with the misplaced confidence of a young teacher, in 1969.

Despite the sceptical tone of much of the above, I honour parts of this earlier tradition, especially as it was practised by teachers like the young Charles Causley. He stumbled on the power of poetry in children's lives by accident. He was once faced, around 1948 (when he was 31) 'with about 80 boys on a Thursday afternoon . . . I used to read them a story . . . all the girls did needlework'.[1] One day he picked up by mistake (he was looking for a story to read) a book of ballads. He told Brian Merrick, many years later:

'I just opened the book ...'

It opened at a poem called *Young Beichan*, and I thought well here goes, and I read:

> *Young Beichan was a noble lord*
> *A lord of high degree*
> *He wente forth to Palestine*
> *Christes tomb for to see ...*

A little boy was sitting in the front row. I can see his face even now. I had to turn over – the first verse was at the bottom of the page – and I turned over two pages and was fumbling a bit, and this boy said, 'Go on then!'. (Merrick, 1989)

I remember reading Causley's poems (*Figgie Hobbin*, 1970) to eight-year-olds in the early seventies, with similar results. I also remember, with gratitude, Causley's painstaking replies to the bundle of letters my class sent him (see Sedgwick, 1999a). More recently, I remember my surprise and delight when I read a four-line poem, 'What are heavy?' by Christina Rossetti, to a class of Year 7 children in my local comprehensive:

> *What are heavy? Sea sand and sorrow.*
> *What are brief? Today and tomorrow.*

[1] Another contemporary shift in attitudes, of course, concerned gender roles. Imagine running a needlework class for girls only after 1965!

Teaching Poetry

What are frail? Spring blossoms and youth.
What are deep? The ocean and truth.

(in Sedgwick, 2002a)

As I finished, I looked up. There was a boy staring at me with a smile on his face; a smile not of mild derision, as I might have expected as a primary school teacher stereotyping the children in the local comprehensive, but of pure pleasure. I can remember his face, as Causley remembered his boy's face. The faces that poetry has enlightened through us stay with us. My boy's face was covered in acne and his hair was, like Timothy Winters' in Causley's justifiably celebrated poem of that name, 'an exclamation mark'. He said two words, the highest terms of praise known, I think, to males of his generation: 'That's cool.'

John Danby's 1940 book *Approach to Poetry* is typical of the best of its period (note, though, its tentative title). It argues the case for poetry as a humanizing influence. It offers advice on how young people can be introduced to poetry. But the most significant sentence in the book is: 'To attain [a] direct relationship between the poem and the reader is the sole end of the poetry lesson.'

The sole end! That phrase seems perverse now, in an age accustomed to (indeed, obsessed with) expressing oneself in the pursuit of emotional health and personal autonomy. To a post-sixties generation, in contrast to Danby's sentence, the 'sole aim' of the poetry lesson is to help children to write their own poems, and that writing is, all too often, isolated from the poems in the traditional canon.

Danby is exactly half right. The relationship of the

'The faces that poetry has enlightened stay with us.'

poem and child that can enable the child to 'approach' questions about mental and spiritual truths and about his or her self and his or her problematic relationships with the world, is vital, and is all but ignored in primary schools today. Great, or even merely good, poetry offers innumerable riches, as long as we pay it due attention. It is sad that many children do not experience their local poetry. Do children in Palmers Green know the poems of their poet Stevie Smith? Are children in Peterborough, close to the birthplace of John Clare, familiar with those of his poems which describe situations that they would recognize? Or, as they sit in their creative writing lessons, are children detached from what their local poets have done?

Danby's book, and Causley's teaching as recalled in Merrick, are exemplary examples of the pre-Beatles, pre-end-of-*Chatterley*-ban, pre-teenager and pre-permissive society approach to poetry. But if you listen to almost anyone recounting his or her experiences of poetry at primary school in those years, you hear different stories. An anecdote of my late grandmother-in-law illustrates the worst of what happened in classrooms before the creative writing revolution. She was a teacher, and she told a class that they were going to do some poetry. She overheard a boy say: 'That means hey nonny no and bloody daffodils.' Almost certainly, somewhere in his head was the memory of having to learn by rote some old-fashioned words that bore (as he saw it, and the pun is intended) no relevance to his life. Michael Benton comments 'In secondary schools, the commonest stock response to poetry is the dismissive groan!' (Benton *et al.*, 1988). In primary schools, too, when the precious nature of poetry was emphasized, this was true. And I deliberately use 'precious', an ambiguous word: to the teacher it meant seeing the poem as 'of great value ... highly esteemed and cherished' (Longmans *Concise English Dictionary*, 1985), while for the child the definition would be (not that he or she would have expressed it in quite these terms) 'excessively refined; affected'.

Another approach to the teaching of poetry was to use it as a handwriting exercise. I remember, circa 1955, a kindly teacher, Mr Ball, writing the first three stanzas of Gray's 'Elegy in a Country Churchyard' on the blackboard, and asking us to copy it out. It was years before I found out how long this poem was, and many more years before I read it all. The first three stanzas were for a long time to my mind like the opening five minutes of the first Tchaikovsky piano concerto, frequently played on the *Light Programme* to end record request programmes: when I discovered that there was another 40 minutes or so, I was appalled. After I bought a recording of the concerto, and discovered that lovely tune was never repeated, and that the rest of the piece was a soup of unrelated material (I hear it very differently now), I felt much the same. That was how I felt when I first saw the 'Elegy' in its entirety.

I see poetry reduced to handwriting today. Children spend half-hours copying a poem about, say, rain. They then have to beautify their copies with illustrations that obscure the writing. The resulting blue diagonal lines reduce the status of the poem even further. What are teachers teaching when they ask children to copy out poems in 'your best writing'?

'What are teachers teaching when they ask children to copy out poems in "your best writing"?'

First, they are teaching children that a poem is a tool for the relatively low status skill of neat handwriting; that poetry comes a long way below calligraphy. They are teaching them to associate poetry with an aching wrist. They are teaching them that poetry by itself is not enough and that it has to be tarted up with coloured crayons.

I can look further back into the twentieth century. My mother gave me glimpses of the way poetry was taught in Eire in the twenties and thirties. As I grew up she was fond of reciting poems, and I am now very grateful that she did. Longfellow's 'The Dying Slave', Hood's 'I Remember', Goldsmith's 'The Village Blacksmith' and the opening of Gray's 'Elegy' (again) were typical examples. She did it in a sing-song voice, over-reliant on the metric count, and detached from natural speech rhythms. She showed no active response to poetry, as we put it today; but she had an appreciation of its beauty, or at least a part of its beauty. I wish I could talk to her now about the teaching of the poetry she experienced.

After the early sixties, as schoolboys searched through *Lady Chatterley's Lover* looking for the good bits, and girls screamed at concerts and in airports as the Fab Four performed or landed, almost all books on poetry concentrated on the writing of it. The world had changed. Marjorie Langdon's 1961 book *Let the Children Write* was a harbinger of the new movement in classrooms, and serves as an exemplar. I remember reading her account of a lesson when she asked children to close their eyes and imagine a spider moving. Then she asked them to write about it. I taught this lesson enthusiastically, unworried about

9

any arachnophobes there might be in class; then, after someone pointed this potential problem out, I did the same lesson, but with cats as the subject. Langdon's work emphasized close attention to the subject, the need to look and look again. This looking was not at something that was physically present in the classroom (although that would have worked as well) but at something that could, with good teaching, be imagined in the child's mind's eye. Later, I learned to teach this looking in tandem with drawing (Sedgwick, 2002b) and that to draw and to write were closely related, as is powerfully shown in Leonardo's notebooks (see especially Richter, 1980).

Sandy Brownjohn's three books (1980, 1982, 1989), with their uniform subtitle 'Teaching Children to Write Poetry', were for many the most influential books of this movement. Other works, by writers like Pie Corbett and Brian Moses (1986), added to the gaiety of classrooms committed to the teaching and learning of poetry. Although these books were essentially collections of proven recipes and had little to say about why the food was pleasurable or nutritional, it should be noted that all these writers suggested that teachers offer children experiences of other poetry before they wrote their own. Brownjohn uses Louis MacNeice, Edward Thomas and traditional verse, and is a passionate advocate of traditional forms. See her informative *The Poet's Craft* (2002) (though prosody on its own is a dry affair). Corbett and Moses use more modern poetry, like Adrian Henri and the ubiquitous 'Warning' by Jenny Joseph.

I remember teaching creative writing. I thought I was doing it well; but I was doing it badly. I slammed adjectives, collected from the brightest children, on the blackboard. I hoped that they wouldn't all use the same ones. But I also hoped, I suppose, that the less able would catch something from the ideas of the more able. I banged on about alliteration, and got results like:

> *The licking flames flickering like fireworks*
> *Dancing among the charred grass*
> *Of the numb November night . . .*

It was characteristic of these lessons that I had read no poems to the children first. Certainly, I did often read poems to them, but such sessions were usually little ten-minute slots just before hometime, lunchtime or playtime. They acted as small sacraments of pleasure, moments almost out of time, in which my relationships with children who had misbehaved were repaired, and in which the children implicitly forgave me for lapses in sympathy and patience. They were not part of the lighting-up period before they wrote. The strange detachment of the teaching of the writing of poetry from the reading of it to children is one of the reasons for my writing this.

It was also characteristic of those lessons that the children used present participles ('flickering', etc.). They shied away from main verbs. Present participles are vague and let the writer off the hook of commitment, while main verbs make things happen. Adjectives also weighed the writing down, in the same way as water weighs down a leaky boat. (Amazingly, some writers on teaching poetry still advise the use of 'more interesting adjectives' in children's poems.)

11

Teaching Poetry

Poetic, in this context, meant unreal, detached from the world and the children's experience of it, as well as from the world of poetry as written by writers in the canon. It meant soft-edged rather than hard-edged: no wonder a character in a Saul Bellow modern novel, *Humbolt's Gift*, characterized poetry as 'a skirt thing, a church thing' (cited in Amis, 1986). Listening to lessons like these, you could feel that (to use Danby's phrase) the sole end of the poetry lesson was to get children writing a poem without knowing anything about poetry; a logical impossibility, of course.

Alec Clegg edited a book in 1963, not exclusively concerned with poetry, that sums up the early sixties insistence on the value of what children can write. It is a marvellous book, with examples of children's verse, typical of the best of the time:

The Candle
White polish; sour milk.
Delicate finger wrapped in a cotton blanket.
Star growing, bigger, bigger flickering in darkness,
A great Lord, now a humble person bowing.
Golden crystals, dark eye,
Slowly, flowing, running, milk.
Faint glimmer of hope, trying to enlarge itself.
Black burned pie; all beauty gone.

(Girl, aged 10)

This is a kenning, a list poem dependent on the teaching of metaphors derived from Anglo-Saxon practice, and it is very good one. But there is no account of the teacher teaching a poem first.

The Larkin poem that I quoted at the beginning of the introduction is relevant to my argument, because the change from 'appreciating great poetry' to 'teaching creative writing' was a sixties phenomenon, along with John Lennon's cocky irreverence, *Oz* magazine and marijuana. The notion that self-expression, by whatever means, was everything, and that taking knowledge from the past was at best an irrelevance, and at worst a kind of intellectual tyranny, manifested itself in some schools – but there were not as many as some commentators on the right believe, or pretend to believe. The progressive movement in education only just inched out of the pages of the *Plowden Report* (a study of primary schools that concluded child-centred methods based on 'discovery learning' were the most effective). It was more dominant in poetry jamborees at the Albert Hall, among other places, which represented a wicked sentimentalism. In fact, the tyrannical notion is that poetry is merely self-expression, and this often leads to demagogic control masked as charismatic posturing. The idea that the poetry of the past is there for all children to use for pleasure, and to help them (perhaps) to write – that is a truly democratic view.

As I have noted, few schools were, in fact, seduced by all this kaftan'd sentimentalism. Most carried on in the old way, using dreadful books with titles like *First Aid in English*, which had as little to do with creativity as they did with the tradition of English poetry. In these books, there were passages where every possible punctuation error had been made and the children had to correct each one. The poetry anthology was produced, typically, in four thin books with uniform covers, colours distinguishing poems for

'The notion that self-expression, by whatever means, was everything, and that taking knowledge from the past was at best an irrelevance, and at worst a kind of intellectual tyranny, manifested itself in some schools.'

seven-year-olds from those for eight-years-olds and so on. If you want to see the contrast between the pre-sixties and the post-sixties, compare this kind of book with vibrant collections like Geoffrey Summerfield's marvellous *Junior Voices* series (1970), books that still do not, more than 30 years later, look or feel out of date.

Viewed from the early years of the third millennium, the division between children encountering poetry and trying to write it is illogical, because the two activities are not only linked, but intermeshed. 'We cannot', wrote Tunnicliffe (1984), 'separate and isolate from one another the twin ... activities of reading and writing it', suggesting, as a model, conjoined twins. Trying to separate the two is also inefficient because doing anything that matters (like writing poetry) is difficult, and so we require all the help we can get (from reading it). If Shakespeare, John Clare and Emily Dickinson (three writers I regularly use in poetry-writing lessons) are freely available to us, we are fools not to use their poems. The following chapters are an attempt to show how indispensable reading poetry is to writing it, and vice versa, and how one way to respond to a poem is to write either in imitation of it, or, even better, in homage to it.

The following chapters are constructed in four main parts. The first chapter looks at children discovering some of the basic elements of poetry in the nursery and on the playground, and listening to poetry in the classroom. The second discusses the ways in which we can help children to make a poem their own, to build bridges between their own feelings, their own lives, and the poem (or the text of a poem). Michael

Teaching Poetry

Benton and his colleagues have written an exceptional and absorbing book about children responding to poetry, and I will draw on their work here.

The third is about children writing their own poetry. The case studies I use here are new. The fourth is a defence of poetry against what R. S. Thomas called 'The Machine'.

1

Children Beginning to Understand Poetry

A world that is too small (R. S. Thomas)

How can a child write a poem if he or she doesn't know what a poem is? You may as well ask him or her to build a sandcastle without ever having been to the Tower of London or to Caernarvon, or, at the very least, having seen a picture of a castle. A student in a department of education told me that she was interested in poetry. 'Whom do you read?' I asked. 'Oh, I don't read much poetry, I'm more interested in writing it', came the reply. I have discussed this weird phenomenon at some length in my book *How to Write Poetry and Get it Published* (2002c), and don't intend to enlarge on it here. But I will add this: there is an extraordinary solipsistic arrogance in thinking that we can create art just because (presumably) our need for self-expression feels so urgent to us. Art that has existed as long as humankind requires rather more than an individual's need to tell readers about his or her failed love affair, or the death of his or her dog.

The first obvious way that adults can help children to understand something basic about the nature of poetry is to read it to them, and to do so as early in their lives as possible. Lucky babies have sensed the

'How can a child write a
poem if he or she
doesn't know what a
poem is?'

rhythms of poetry before they can understand the meanings of words. They do this when they are bounced on a knee: 'Diddle diddle dumpling my son John / Went to bed with his trousers on / Diddle diddle dumpling my son John.'

My Bangalory Man: nursery rhymes

The Opies wrote 'In a child's life there is a period when almost the whole extent of his literature is the *nursery* rhyme' (Opie and Opie, 1955, my emphasis). There are, for most of us who work with children, two problems with this.

One is the common belief that many children today do not know any nursery rhymes. The oral tradition is dead. I suspect that this is just another example of 'fings' – young people's manners, the tunes in pop music, children's knowledge of nursery rhymes – 'not being what they used to be'. I suspect that the oral tradition is, in fact, more alive than many teachers think. Also, the assumption that the computer and Play Station have largely removed, first, folk verse and then the book, from children's early experience – an assumption often expressed to me on my travels to schools – may be part of a middle-class snobbery about working-class homes. It may also (to be frank) be the result of a need on the part of teachers to emphasize the weight of the work they have to do. We do not (the unspoken argument runs) just get the children through SATs. We also have to read them these little proto-poems that decent homes would already have introduced to the children.

Teaching Poetry

The second problem is a class problem, too, and a more justifiable one: the very word 'nursery' has been out of use even in upper-middle-class homes (I think) for many years, and has never (I know) had a place among the more lowly of us. I can dimly recall it alienating me when I was a child. In the little council flat where I was brought up, I thought of a nursery as a book-lined room with oak chests full of toys, a nanny and a visiting tutor. This place couldn't have been further from the small bedroom I had to myself, where the seed-bed of my library was laid in a cupboard, among my school blazer and black trousers and (later) my jeans; all this as late as my seventeenth year.

I want to suggest the term of 'folk rhyme', instead of 'nursery rhyme'. It suits the rhymes the Opies collected, but it also fits another kind of rhyme that I am going to discuss later in this section: the playground rhyme. The difference between the two is that nursery rhymes sound, or read, as if they were composed (if not actually written) by adults. They date mostly from the sixteenth, seventeenth and eighteenth centuries, and were, it seems, composed for adult entertainment (how soiled that phrase has become!). Playground rhymes, on the other hand, seem to come directly from the informal committee that the worldwide childhood tribe has set up for this purpose. You can see the papers this committee has produced in books by Hallworth (1994), Rosen and Steele (1982), and others, and later on in this section.

Many adults either dislike or ignore poetry. Some hate it. But most of us, as children, listening to nursery rhymes, adored it. Maybe we can't remember adoring it, but it is almost certain that we laughed at the constant repetition of lines like this:

Georgie Porgie pudding and pie
Kissed the girls and made them cry;
When the boys came out to play
Georgie Porgie ran away.

These words, and thousands of others, hang around for life in our brains. They may not be what a sophisticated adult calls poetry, but they are the first shoots. They appeal to what the Opies call a child's 'inborn musical fancy'. The child responds to what Cowley (quoted in Opie and Opie, 1959) calls 'the tinkling of the rime and the dance of the numbers'. They are to poetry what the child kicking a football in a street is to the man scoring a winning goal in the World Cup. When they listen to rhymes like this, and when their parents bounce them rhythmically to them, children learn something of the rudiments of poetry – rhythm and rhyme and structure – long before they know these terms. Teachers who are not sure what an internal rhyme is have not noticed that one of their first poems – 'Georgie Porgie' – begins with a perfect example.

Also, this verse speaks of a universal situation. It may be difficult, but it is not impossible, for us to speculate on it. Who is Georgie, with his pudding and his pie? Why does he kiss the girls? Why does he run away from the boys? Some say that he is the Prince Regent, later George IV, and that the verses refer, none too delicately, to his amorous adventures. A generation later, some of us repeated those lines with a new, now politically incorrect, last line: 'He kissed them too. He's funny that way'. By doing that, we were already being creative. We were making things, and we were subverting the original.

Young people's undermining of what they are expected to enjoy is an important element in the beginnings of the awareness of poetry. To take the first line of the well-known Christmas hymn, for example, and change it into 'While shepherds washed their socks by night . . . ' is a staging post (a very early one, admittedly) on the road to understanding that poetry is not only there to reinforce what we already know. It exists, at least in part, to subvert what we know; to lead on to knowing something else; to understand that everything is provisional; that things are never definitively in order, as most hymns ('The rich man in his castle, the poor man at his gate') would insist they were.

'Georgie Porgie' is, of course, familiar. Here is a less well-known example which I, for one, did not know in my childhood:

Follow my Bangalorey Man;
Follow my Bangalorey Man;
I'll do all that I ever can
To follow my Bangalorey Man.
We'll borrow a horse, and steal a gig,
And round the world we'll do a jig
And I'll do all that I ever can
To follow my Bangalorey Man.

(Opie and Opie, 1955)

For me, the rediscovery of nursery rhymes was a weird freedom. To find a piece like that, for example, set so many resonances bouncing in my mind. Some were religious. Some were romantic. Who is the speaker? A girl expressing devotion to her lover; possibly one banned by her parents? Is she like the girls in those folksongs who ran off with 'gypsy rovers'?

Or is she a religious devotee? Is the Bangalorey Man a kind of messiah, or a kind of fraud? There is a clue, I suppose, to the provenance of these verses in the similarity of the word to the name of the Indian city Bangalore, but this does not stop my imagination roaming beyond that. These verses, at their best, have an incantatory quality. There is a hint of magic behind them: they might make something happen; something not for the good of everybody. Auden bluntly puts it like this: 'poetry is sin' (in the dedicatory poem of the *Collected Poems*, 1976).

This hint of magic, which draws all children to rhymes like these, may be one of the reasons why so many adult humans hate poetry and insist on having nothing to do with it. Perhaps, in Ted Hughes' lovely phrase they are 'deaf / to the intelligence of heaven' (Hughes, 1997); perhaps they are fundamentalist in some religious or secular way, and so refuse to see beyond what their senses or their narrow view of the world allows them to see. They glimpse in poetry the possibility of sin, without understanding the inevitability of it, let alone its possible redemption.

The Opies included this next poem in a section of their book called 'Awakenings', when 'a new, almost adult tone begins to pervade the verse. Here, perhaps, is the first hint of poetry ...'.

How many miles to Babylon?
Three-score and ten.

23

Can I get there by candle-light?
Yes, and back again.
If your heels are nimble and light,
You may get there by candle-light.

Because of its familiarity, that rhyme usually passes us by without our noticing it. To read it slowly, however, opens up many possibilities. What is it about? Here is a provisional list of its subjects: journeys; the exile of the Jews in the Old Testament; three-score and ten, the biblical lifetime; candle-light; bedtime; the words 'if' and 'may' and their implied risk: nothing is certain.

If we want to introduce children to poetry, we need to remember our own childhood experiences of nursery rhymes, and reinvigorate that experience with our adult understanding, before asking the children about what they know and understand.

Playground rhymes

But there is something that children do that is at least potentially poetic without the dubious assistance of adults. I hinted at this in the last section, when I quoted that new version of 'Georgie Porgie', and suggested a category of verses that might include both nursery rhymes and playground rhymes, 'folk poetry'.

I write 'children' there, but I mean 'girls', because boys seem to be less interested in playground rhymes. They collect around the girls when the girls are telling me rhymes, and they are amused by what

24

f we want to introduce children to poetry, we need to remember our own childhood experiences of nursery rhymes, and reinvigorate that experience with our adult understanding.'

they hear. But they have nothing to contribute. I have memories of rhymes from my own boyhood: aggressively sexual doggerel, mostly, that I am too embarrassed to type here, and this memory leads me to suspect that boys today have similar material that, in today's political climate, they, too, are embarrassed, or even ashamed, by.

Respecting the poetry girls say, or sing, in the playground, is one way of laying the foundations of poetry for children. The rhythms will recur in the classroom. Making a collection of the children's rhymes of different cultures shows them that they are part of a huge and successful tribe, and this helps them to respect themselves and their fellow citizens all over the world. I have been collecting rhymes for over 30 years, but I have never (who has?) attacked the subject with the academic rigour and astonishing passion for the demotic that Iona and Peter Opie have. Any reader wanting to dig further into the earth around the roots of children's appreciation of poetry is directed to two timeless books by the Opies, *The Lore and Language of Schoolchildren* (1959) and *The Singing Game* (1988).

Here is a sample from my shoebox:

Abna Babna
Lady Snee
Ocean potion
Sugar and tea
Potato roast and English toast
And out goes she.

(Caribbean, Guyana)

26

Hokey pokey winky wum
How do you like your taties done?
Snip snap snorum
Hi popalorum
Kate go scratch it
You are OUT!

(Scottish)

I've lost my love
And I do not care,
I've lost my love
And I do not care,
I'll soon have another one
Better than the other one
I've lost my love
And I do not care.

(England)

And I keep singing in my heart
Don't mark me late
Don't mark me late

(England, Liverpool)

No more Latin
No more French
No more sitting on the old school bench
 (Caribbean, but widespread in different versions)

One two three O'Leary
I saw Kate McLeary
Sitting on her bumbaleary
Eating chocolate biscuits.

(Scotland)

Teaching Poetry

Poppa Moishe killed a skunk
Mamma Moishe cooked a skunk
Babba Moishe ate a skunk
Oh my goodness how they stunk!

(USA)

It is important to show children that the elements of poetry are contained in these rhymes. They have, for example, an exuberant use of language: alliteration is there (not introduced officially, I am told, in the UK until Year 5, when children are ten years old), rhythm and metre are also present, along with rhyme. Repetition reinforces the playfulness of such rhymes, and anticipates the playfulness of much poetry (you can't be a poet without playing with language). These rhymes have surprises built into them, just as all good poetry must have an element of surprise (otherwise, it would be composed of cliché, that most anti-poetic thing).

Some of these verses also show intense feeling. 'And I keep singing in my heart / Don't make me late / Don't make me late' is my favourite example. That verses like this come to birth mysteriously and grow, equally mysteriously, all over the world – this strange fact should alert us to the existence of that tribe, in one way intimately known, in another way not known at all, the tribe of children. To know that tribe we have to get down on 'hands and knees, / The adult subterfuge ... / [and] probe and pry / With analytic eye. (R. S. Thomas again, from 'Children's Song'); and still understand that we won't truly understand it, but simply have to regret what we knew when we were children, which we have forgotten.

And there is a problem with these rhymes. While it

28

is important to recognize their significance, it is also important not to appropriate these rhymes to our prying officialdom, our 'analytic eye'. Many books – such as those by Michael Rosen and Susanna Steele (1982), and Grace Hallworth (1994) – take this risk. The former collection manages to print rude verses and, at the same time, sanitize them with an unerring and determined 'right-on-ness'. You wonder, as you read it, to whom do these rhymes belong?

I wrote to six schools asking them to do some research into the rhymes of previous generations. Middleton, in Suffolk, responded with a note from Sue Abbott:

I remember saying this when I was little:

> Teddy Bear, Teddy Bear, turn around
> Teddy Bear, Teddy Bear, touch the ground
> Teddy Bear, Teddy Bear, go upstairs
> Teddy Bear, Teddy Bear, say your prayers
> Teddy Bear, Teddy Bear, switch off the light
> Teddy Bear, Teddy Bear, say goodnight.

Two people hold the rope skipping, person in the middle jumping does the actions whilst skipping, i.e., touch the ground, pretend to go upstairs, hold hands together for prayers, pretend to switch off the light . . .

One of the teachers in the same school, Annie Clark, remembered the same rhyme, but with 'Ballerina' substituted for 'Teddy bear'. She performed her version for the children, much to their (and my) surprised delight.

An anonymous correspondent sent me this oddity:

Have you ever ever ever
In your long-legged life
Seen a long-legged sailor
With a long-legged wife?

No I've never never never
In my long-legged life
Seen a long-legged sailor
With a long-legged wife.

I noted three elements of poetry: repetition, playfulness and rhyme. And another contribution came from 'Megan's Grandma' who was a child in Lancashire in the 1920s:

A soul cake
A soul cake
Please good Missus
A soul cake
An apple a pair a plum or a cherry
Any good thing to make us merry
One for Peter one for Paul
And one for him who made us all
A soul cake

This rhyme was sung by children in pre-Christmas week. They carried cups – soul-cups – and they received a piece of fruit from a kind of punch as a thank you for their song, together with a soul cake, like a small cake.

(Megan's Mother)

Reading poetry to children

This part of the book is comprised of advice based on long experience of reading poetry to children, both at

30

Children Beginning to Understand Poetry

Key Stage 1 and Key Stage 2, and of helping them to enjoy its music and meaning. This is the first place where children in schools can begin to respond to poems that go beyond their nursery rhyme, playground and street experiences.

The first point to make is about the 'poetry voice'. Oh, the poetry voice – that special, precious way of reading poetry to children, over-reliant on the metre, that so drives children (and adults) away from poetry. What is it like? I can't describe it. I wish I had a CD to go with this section, featuring Norma, a composite figure made up of several teachers I have known, reading poetry to her children: 'Now children, I am going to read some Poetry [n.b. you can hear the capital P, and precious pronunciation that distorts 'oe' into something like 'oy'] to you [long pause while the children express their gratitude by offering gifts of gin, chocolates and cash. Actually, some version of 'hey nonny no and bloody daffodils' is going through their heads] ... I want you to listen very, very hard...Are you listening?... Jonathan, are you listening?'

And that is just the intro. Why do we need a poetry voice? Can't poetry speak for itself? Norma doesn't say 'Now children we are going to do some science/physical education ...': she just gets on with it. Why can't she just get on with poetry? It is probably because of a vestigial belief somewhere inside her mind that sees poetry as essential quasi-religious, and also frail, and, like Chopin in T. S. Eliot's 'Portrait of a Lady', not to be 'rubbed and questioned in the concert room' or anywhere else. When Philip Larkin came across the poetry of Hardy, he was grateful that Hardy taught him that he didn't have to 'jack himself up' to some higher plane.

Norma is still at the stage, poetry-wise, where she believes it is some special thing, holy in an undefined way, and liable to be shattered in the hurly-burly of everyday life.

And how does Norma read the poem? Her sing-song method insists that poetry is nothing to do with the world we live in. In a voice that she never uses in the pub (I once watched her drink a Dubonnet and lime), or while ordering fish and chips (I haven't tested this), or when arguing about politics (I have done this many times), the way she speaks infers a kind of debased heaven (or, in a word, hell) where all speech is a dishonest poetry, and all poetry is a dishonest speech.

What about the opposite to this, the everyday voice, the voice that tries to ignore the metre, and everything that is conventionally supposed to be poetic? Reading poetry to children requires both the magical – the numinous – and the everyday. The difficult gap between the two is a tension that poetry in the classroom (or anywhere) cannot do without. The wrestle between the length of lines and the length of sentences, and between rhyme and normal speech, must be explored as we read a poem. This tension is apparent when we read a poem like Robert Frost's 'Birches'. It famously begins:

> *When I see birches bend to left and right*
> *Across the lines of straighter darker trees,*
> *I like to think some boy's been swinging them ...*

The lines are clearly based on the iambic pentameter, but they have a casual, spoken-voice quality. Recast them as prose:

'Reading poetry to children requires both the magical – the numinous – and the everyday.'

*When I see birches bend to left and right across
the lines of straighter darker trees, I like to think
some boy's been swinging them...*

Although this reads perfectly, the verse can still be
discerned in there, like a ghost. This exemplifies the
tension we need between speech and verse rhythms
when we read to children. It is not a matter of mid-point
between the two, of flabby compromise, but of writer,
and reader exploiting the tension between the two
rhythms.

The poems we chose

One problem in teaching poetry is that many children
leave their primary schools thinking that poetry has to
be funny. This is understandably so, because the diet
they are offered is so frequently facetious. Looking
along the poetry shelves of my local Waterstones, I
pick titles at random: *Silly Verse*, *Time for a Rhyme*,
Pimples on my Bum. These are books that sell
poetry, with its ability to help human beings to enjoy
and endure, fearsomely short. There are fine poets who
are interested in the demotic. Indeed, all poets have an
interest in everyday language.

But decent poets, like Allan Ahlberg and Michael
Rosen, are only part of the picture. The poetry
shelves are filled by the yelping voices of those who
would appeal to the children, or so they say, but really
only appeal (or try to appeal) to the market traders, the
publishers, and what they think children want. Children
enjoy the solemn and the serious as well as the light
and frivolous. Here is my friend Beth reading to her

infants. In her lesson, she uses both the demotic and
the traditional, but never the patronizing. The children
go quiet as Beth looks around expectantly. She says:
'Thank you, Edward, Caroline, for being so quiet.' The
others easily take the hint. Then, without any preamble,
she says:

Elsie Marley's grown so fine
She won't get up to feed the swine
But stays in bed till eight or nine!
Lazy Elsie Marley!

As she says the word 'lazy', her eyes widen with
mock, or perhaps real (it's hard to tell), shock. She
does not ask the children about the poem, but, after a
moment's silence and a questioning look, she asks a
child to help her say a poem: 'Stephanie, will you say
"NO!" in a naughty voice when I point at you please.'
The result is:

New Girl

Out you crawl Aleisha from
under the water tray –
NO!

  Aleisha Brown the new girl
  runs the school today.

Down you come Aleisha
from the climbing frame –
NO!

  Who's in charge of school today?
  Aleisha is her name.

> *Leave that boy Aleisha,*
> *he's done you no harm –*
> *NO!*
>
>> *Aleisha's in a fighting mood –*
>> *Sound the alarm!*
>
> *That lady's the headteacher,*
> *Aleisha! Put her down! . . .*
> *NO!*
>
>> *Assembly will be led today*
>> *by Miss Aleisha Brown.*
>
> *NO!*

This is my poem, so I have a vested interest in being pleased to hear it read, and read well. It is light, of course, but it has a truth in it that all teachers of infants and, indeed, all infants, instantly recognize. In every group of reception children there is at least one child who, in sociological jargon, is not yet socialized; who, in conventional terms, is naughty; and who, in broader terms, is still a free spirit.

As Beth reads other poems, within this lovely haven (well, I like being there) of verbal pleasure, children react in different ways. Malcolm is statemented, and has either 'severe learning difficulties' (as the educational psychologist has put it). Or he is dyslexic (as his parents have put it). Malcolm mouths the words as Beth reads, and smiles broadly as she finishes.

So far the poems have been light in tone. But from now on, Beth mixes things a little. She has a battered, brown-paper-wrapped copy of Charles Causley's *Collected Poems for Children* (1970). She alternates the uproarious 'I saw a jolly hunter' with the sombre and chilling 'By St Thomas Water'; the cheerful 'Lucy Love's Song' with 'Rise up Jenny', a poem that, like several by Causley, questions the world's assumption that 'the lion's share / Of happiness is found by couples' (Larkin).

One important aspect of Beth's lesson is that it only lasts 15 minutes at the most. Another is that, even when the subject matter of the poems is sombre, the overwhelming feeling of the lesson is pleasurable. It is, as I have said, a little sacrament of friendship.

Children find poetry, if they are lucky, with their parents; and then, lucky or not, they find a version of it in their playgrounds and, one hopes, with their teachers. Later, perhaps, they learn to respond to it, to make individual poems their own.

'If we mean to help
children to respond to
poems more strongly,
we should practise such
responses ourselves.
How can we teach what
we have not learnt?'

2
Children and Teachers Responding to Poetry

The work of Louise Rosenblatt (especially 1978, described in Benton *et al.*, 1988) helps us to understand that 'every time a reader experiences a work of art, it is in a sense created anew . . . the process of understanding implies a re-creation of it'. A more traditional formula than Rosenblatt's would be this one:

Reader _ poem

Rosenblatt, on the other hand, works with this formula:

Reader _ _ _ _ _ _ _ _ poem _ _ _ _ _ _ _ _ text

Within this, the text is merely that: a text, a set of words. The poem doesn't come into existence (or, better still, come alive) until the reader responds to it or (to revert to a phrase I used in the last section), makes it his or hers. The text is like a symphonic musical score that only comes alive when an orchestra plays it. Each reader brings to each poem a different baggage to that of other readers, much as each conductor, each violinist his or hers and, come to that, as each member of the audience brings his or her unique

39

perspective to the concert hall. My past, my mood today, my knowledge of the countryside (or lack of it), my previous experience of poetry in general and the poetry of Gerard Manley Hopkins in particular – all these affect the way I respond to his poem 'Margaret'. 'Reading,' says the great tragic Russian poet Marina Tsvetaeva (quoted in Brodsky, 1987) 'is complicity in the creative process'. T. S. Eliot believed that 'the author's interpretation of his work is no more pertinent than that of the reader. On *The Waste Land* specifically, he told one enquirer that the real meaning of the poem is, 'that which it holds for whoever is reading it' (Ackroyd, 1984). If we believe this, we will read with greater attention than if we see a poem as merely an inert thing on the page.

Play Beethoven's *Pastoral Symphony*: a townie will respond very differently from a country person. Indeed, inside their heads, people will create different pieces of music. Bernard Levin, music critic, once wrote that, as far as he was concerned, the countryside could be concreted over. How did he, as a music-lover, listen to the *Pastoral?* (By the way, I always felt that I would have been pleased had *he* been concreted over.) In *Howard's End* E. M. Forster shows different characters responding in different ways to another Beethoven symphony, the *Fifth*, and thereby making the music their own. Indeed, colluding in its composition:

Mrs Munt [tapped] surreptitiously when the tunes came...Helen [saw] heroes and horses in the music's flood...Margaret [saw] only the music...Tibby, who is profoundly versed in counterpoint...holds the full score open on his knee...Fraulein Mosebach [remembers] all the time that Beethoven is 'echt Deutsch'...Fraulein

Mosebach's young man...can remember nothing but Fraulein Mosebach...

Thus, in its majestic complexity, Beethoven's *Fifth* tells different stories inside the heads of different listeners because they collude in its making. To a later generation, the opening theme (three identical short notes, then a drop to a longer one: 'da-da-da-daa') speaks about victory, because it is the rhythm of the V sign in Morse code, and became emblematic during the Second World War.

A final analogy: I have read Jane Austen's *Pride and Prejudice* every two or three years since I was 20. When I first read it, I was the same age as the heroine, Elizabeth Bennet. I fell in love with her. Now I am even older than her father and there is no-one in the story who is anything like the age I am now. It is cold comfort to know that I bring to my reading of the book an increased understanding of English prose, of Austen's prose in particular, and a more acute psychological understanding of life than I did when I was 20.

I also bring to it experience. Being old, I have more sympathy for Mr Bennet. Paradoxically, I am as much shocked by his moral laxness in wanting to be alone in his library as I am by his wife's grasping, stupid vulgarity. I read the book in a different way. I hear a different story. I am still in love with Elizabeth, but not as a hopeful suitor, but as the father of a grown-up child. I collude with Austen in the making of her novels simply by living and by reading with due attention. More to the point, I also collude with Hopkins in the making of each of his poems: again, simply by living and by reading with due care.

There is a robust and very English rejection of this idea that the 'critic' (as well as, presumably, any reader who is less highly designated – the mere reader) 'might [construe] a poem in a way [the poet] felt [he or she] didn't mean'. Unsurprisingly, it is Philip Larkin who concludes: 'I should think he was talking balls.' This is a robust positivism: a thing is made and that is the end of the matter. I am reminded of Samuel Johnson's presumed (at least by himself) refutation of Bishop Berkeley's denial of the existence of matter: 'I refute it thus' (striking his foot against a stone).

This positivism – of Johnson and of Larkin – would no doubt pick up on that weasely phrase in Rosenblatt: 'in a sense' (only the work of art is created anew).

For the purposes of education, however, Rosenblatt treats children as active learners; and despite current educational orthodoxy, we would be well advised to view children (and, come to that, ourselves as teachers) in the same light.

W. H. Auden's verse works against the orthodoxy that it is necessary to be evangelical about 'this unpopular art'. Auden served poetry, of course, by writing it, but also by the closest kind of reading that is possible. He didn't need to preach. Whether we, as teachers, aspire to be poets or not, we too can serve this art with our reading. If we do not, our teaching will suffer.

Case studies of children responding to poems

Much as I sympathize with English positivism, and admire the poetry of Philip Larkin, and James Boswell's stories about Samuel Johnson, I prefer to see the reader as a more active person than it appears either Larkin or Johnson do. I do not believe that what you can see (or kick) is what you should necessarily believe in. There is no correct view of a poem towards which all readers are striving. A poem does not have what Richards (quoted in Benton *et al.*, 1988) calls a 'plain sense'. Ambiguity is endemic to poetry: if there are no ambiguities in a poem, then it is not a poem. Of course, there are shallow readings of poems, but these are of as little use to the reader as to the poet.

Adults responding to a poem

This is an attempt to show the difference between a shallow reading and one that digs deeper, that is more careful and more strenuous. You may question the necessity, in a book about teaching poetry, of a passage about teachers reading closely, but if we mean to help children to respond to poems more strongly, we should practice such responses ourselves. How can we teach what we have not learnt?

Read this poem three times; once, quickly, then twice more with increasing attention, the third time moving your lips as you read, in order to taste the words. The identity of the poet is not important:

Neutral Tones
We stood by a pond that winter day,
And the sun was white, as though chidden of God,
And a few leaves lay on the starving sod;
They had fallen from an ash, and were gray.

Teaching Poetry

Your eyes on me were as eyes that rove
Over tedious riddles of long ago;
And some words played between us to and fro
  On which lost the more by our love.

The smile on your mouth was the deadest thing
Alive enough to have strength to die;
And a grin of bitterness swept thereby
  Like an ominous bird a-wing.

Since then, keen lessons that love deceives,
And wrings with wrong, have shaped to me
Your face, and the God-cursed sun, and a tree,
  And a pond edged with grayish leaves.

I suggest that you make jottings on that poem. Next, look particularly at the following elements in the poem (this exercise is best done in a group, with each member studying the poem and answering the questions, followed by a discussion).

1. Diction; above all, words concerned with what the title calls 'neutral tones'.

2. Rhyme.

3. Movement of the lines.

4. Diction again: what do you notice about the nouns?

5. Alliteration.

6. Diction, in the third stanza, especially the nouns.

Dawn's response

I asked Dawn, who is a voracious reader of fiction but not of poetry, to jot down her initial reactions to this in line with Benton's suggestions:

[T]alk about the poem in any way they pleased but at some point to consider 1) what the poem was about 2) how it said what it was saying 3) any things they liked or disliked about it 4) why they felt as they did about it.

(Peter Benton, quoted in M. Benton *et al.*, 1988)

and then in line with mine as outlined above.

She notes memory first: 'Memory informs memory ... a memory isn't just a memory, it's other memories of that memory, which distort the original truth of a situation ... but the description here is vivid, even though the event took place "years ago".' Dawn picks up the notion of death ('the person will die') and links this with her experience as a worker in hospices, and with the lines 'Alive enough to have strength to die' (she says, 'you have to have strength to die'). She picks out the following words in response to my first question (about words connected to the title): 'white', 'starving', 'ash', 'gray', 'fallen', 'tedious', 'deadest', 'die' and 'grayish'. The movement of the lines suggest to her a 'to and fro' movement between 'that winter day', 'years ago' (before the winter day) and 'now'.

My responses

I had not picked up on memory, or the idea that there were three stages in the poem rather than two. Nor had

I thought that the woman in the poem might be dead. But then I lack the experience Dawn brings to the poem and, in particular, the line 'Alive enough to have strength to die'. I had far longer to do this exercise than Dawn: I have been reading the poem for twenty-odd years, and I shall almost certainly go on returning to the poem for the rest of my life: that is, in part, what making a poem 'mine' is.

This poem is about the end of a love affair. This is a common subject for poetry, and all kinds of lyric: think of all the songs with 'it's over' in the title. My baggage includes songs by Roy Orbison and Cliff Richard: others will bring different songs to the discussion. To mention them is not to say that they share the complexity of the 'Neutral Tones', or the subtlety, or the craftsmanship.

In this poem, the ending has probably been mooted by one or other of the characters more than once before: 'Parting, after about five / Rehearsals ... ' as Larkin wryly puts it in 'Wild Oats'. The poet presents what he has to say about this situation with heaps of neutral words, a flattish metric. In answer to my own list of questions, I wrote:

1. I count at least three: 'neutral' itself, 'gray' (emphasized by rhyme 'day' and 'ash'; although other words – 'tedious' and 'edged' are in this category).

2. In particular the sudden descent from 'chidden' (it was nearly 'children'!) 'of God' to 'starving sod' – but also the way 'day' becomes 'gray' or vice versa.

3. The metre feels dead to me, and thus enacts the incipient death of the relationship described.

Perhaps other readers won't feel this. Robert Gittings (1978), the poet's biographer, for example, hears in the metre 'the shorter and more varied lines ... [flickering] and [playing] over the scene like the emotions of the unhappy pair ...'.

4. Many of the verbs are inert: 'stood'; 'was'; 'lay'; 'die'. Even the verbs of movement are, given the context, unadventurous: 'rove', for example.

5. 'W': 'winter' day, 'white' sun – both pictures are emphasized by the picked up 'w' in 'words', and visually the unsounded 'w' in 'wrings' and 'wrongs', words alliterated as 'r' words; that repeated 'r' emphasizes the implicit violence of 'wring' (like a neck).

6. The way the 'smile' is not only 'dead' but the 'dead-est thing'; the way 'strength' modulates to 'die'; the way that 'smile' becomes (like a skeleton's smile) a 'grin'.

Later, I noticed other things. The phrase 'chidden of God' is picked up in the last stanza with 'God-curst'. The alliterative use of the letter 'w' throughout the poem is anticipated in the first word. The dreary word 'pond'. (from the Middle English 'ponde', an artificially confined body of water) is used both in the first and last lines of the poem.

To look at a poem in this way is not to look for 'plain sense'. It is to acknowledge ambiguity, and the significance of our own baggage on our reading of poems and, thus, our collusion in their making. It is to look for truth. As teachers, we should first try, by careful close reading, to make each poem our own and second try to help the children to make each poem their own. Benton's technique is an excellent starting-point for this. Perhaps my questions can be usefully asked at a later stage in the lesson.

I do not usually include biographical material in discussion of individual poems. There are three good reasons for this. First there is no guarantee that a poet's 'I' in a poem is him or herself. Many poets are, after all, writing fiction. See, especially, Browning: his great work, 'My Last Duchess', in which the speaker listens to an autocratic, princely murderer talk about the death of his young innocent wife, is an example of a poem that must be seen, among other things, as a short story. Even a poem that uses 'I' consistently is not necessarily speaking the thoughts of the poet.

Second, the poem, which supplies less information than a story or a novel, works detached from the biographical material of that poet. This is connected to the third reason, that reading poems for the assumed autobiographical content detracts attention from the work of art the artist is making, and in which the reader is colluding.

Despite this, I cannot help noting that this mournful poem, which seems to be written from a position near the end of a life, was, in fact, composed when the poet was only 27 years old. 'Neutral Tones' is an early poem by Thomas Hardy.

To read a poem in this way is not to 'dissect' it, to pull it apart and look at the pieces; nor, worse, to vivisect it, to kill it by pulling it apart. The popular view that the activity I have described takes the magic out of a poem depends on a sentimental idea of what poetry is, and stems from the last shoots of romanticism. You can glimpse it when Gerty MacDowell (in *Ulysses*, Joyce, 1993) thinks of the poetry she might write ('Art though real / my ideal?').

Other poems that I have used with university students in education departments to teach close reading include four by Seamus Heaney: 'Blackberry-Picking' and 'Digging' from *Death of a Naturalist* (1966), and 'The Rain Stick' and 'Two Lorries' from *The Spirit Level* (1996). If I were to choose one book as a source for stimulating close reading it would be Seamus Heaney's and Ted Hughes's *The Rattle Bag* (Heaney and Hughes, 1982). It is a glorious book, but, more importantly in this context, it bridges the gap between poetry for children and poetry for adults. Flipping through *The Rattle Bag* now, I cannot find a single poem that will not repay this sort of reading.

Children reading poems closely

The author is talking about a war but using flowers and people to explain it. (Kirsty, aged 11)

The germ of this idea, which is concerned with teaching both the reading and the writing of poetry, comes from Sandy Brownjohn's 1982 book. She describes how she offered the children in her class a prose paraphrase of Edward Thomas's famous poem 'Adlestrop'. She deliberately makes every detail in the poem vague: the lines '... willows, willow-herb, and grass / And meadowsweet and haycocks dry' become, in her account, 'some grass and a couple of different sorts of wild flowers'. She then asked her children to make a poem out of her prose. Following Brownjohn, I gave the children a woolly version of another poem. Here is my prose, even worse than that of Brownjohn:

Poem to remember someone by (Spring religious festival concerned with death and rebirth 1915)

The colourful plants, that are still there when end
*   of day comes in the woodland area*
at the time of this spring religious festival
*   concerned*
with death and rebirth, remind me of the male
*   human beings*
who are a long way from their houses and land,
*   and who, with their girlfriends, might*
have been picking them, and won't pick them,
*   not for ever and ever.*

Perhaps my readers might like to try this exercise: make that woolly prose into verse as concisely as you can.

I gave the children my version of the poem. It is bad prose, of course, but I have carefully arranged it in the four-line form of the original. One characteristic of poetry is concision, and my prose (as Brownjohn's did) lacked that to an obvious, indeed comical extent. I changed 'men' to 'male human beings' for example, expecting the children to write 'men' – but they had a choice of 'boys' or 'lads', and some of the more alert children might find 'soldiers', from a hint later on: the men are no longer around to pick flowers. Also, I

50

changed 'Easter' and 'flowers' into similarly bloated phrases.

Here are some of the children's poems from the first time that I taught this lesson:

Roses that grow in the woods
Easter remind me of men.
Faraway from their lovers might
Never pick them again.

(Jenny)

This poem fortuitously found Thomas's 'men/again' rhyme. Lorna, the teacher, rather sceptically asked her learning support assistant (LSA), when I picked this poem out from the pile, 'How much did you help with this?' The reply was 'Hardly at all ... I had nothing to do with the rhymes'. She added, on my querying this: 'I never noticed them.' The child was seen as a pupil who required the help of an LSA, but she had produced four gnomic, if botanically improbable, little lines that pulled me up short. Her grammar, of course, was unconventional. But so often is that of Shakespeare, and conservative educationists, obsessed with both the Bard and what they deem 'correct', should note this.

All the children found Thomas's complex syntax a problem. As I read it again, I note how his poem is composed of one sentence, and a much longer one than most children will have encountered in prose, let alone verse, by the age of 10. There is the main clause, two subordinate clauses and two subordinate phrases. '[T]hem' in the last line refers back to the second word of the poem, and this is a long distance even for an experienced reader when encountering this poem for the first time. For the 10- and 11-year-olds, it led to grammatical confusion. But this confusion should not detract from what a child like Jenny got from the poem.

Thomas was unique among the children in not keeping to the four-line structure:

The flowers which still stand
There in the sunlit forest
At the time of the Easter party
Men who fled from their properties
With the beloved one who
Have been taken the flowers, and will
Never take them ever again.

While Jenny had simply ignored my 'houses and land' phrase, Thomas had translated it into 'properties', something I would not have dreamed of any child using. Was he hearing subconsciously the sounds of 'party'? Or is one of his parents an estate agent?

Melissa also ignored my 'houses and land', but produced a moving last line:

The roses are still there at nightfall in the bushes
The time
Of Easter celebrations.
Distant, families are picking no more.

Jasmin was the first writer to move into unpredictable diction, with her 'ventured':

'Whether these poems are any good, by whatever criterion, is beside the point. The real issue is the quality of learning, by which I mean the quality of the mental and imaginative processes through which the children went as they wrote.'

Teaching Poetry

The primroses that are still there when night
*   comes in the bush*
At the time of Easter remind me of men
Who have ventured far from their homes with their
*   lovers*
Who might be taking them and won't be not ever.

Whether these poems are any good, by whatever criterion, is beside the point of a book like this. The real issue is the quality of learning, by which I mean the quality of the mental and imaginative processes through which the children went as they wrote. I am not concerned with the extent to which the children have met externally imposed objectives. Such objectives, or targets, would be difficult to conceptualize, as they are about any really demanding task.

What are these children learning as they write? They are having an intense struggle with language. They are learning about themselves, about their world, about the relationship between themselves and that world, about language, and about poetry.

Later, I gave teachers on a course – all English graduates – the same prose paraphrase. The first resulting verse is by Lesley, an English adviser:

Bluebells in the evening wood
At Easter time when men
Now far away might have come with girls
But picked them, but never, never will.

Lesley lamented her choice of 'girls' when she saw the original (see p. 55). Helen, a teacher, wrote:

(see p. 55)

Bluebells in the forest twilight
Are Easter reminders of our men
Far away from home and lovers; unable now
And forever, to pick them.

Lisa, another teacher, could not decide on certain words, and wrote:

Sunset in the woods/forest
Easter daffodils (call to mind/recall) the men
So distant who, with lovers
Might have picked them, but never can/will.

All the writers, children and teachers, except for Thomas, felt it necessary to particularize 'the colourful plants', naming 'bluebells', 'roses', and 'daffodils'. Only one writer, Lisa, felt brave enough to change the order of the elements in my prose version of the poem.

The second part of the lesson began when I gave the children the original poem typed on sheets of A4, and therefore with plenty of space around it. Here, at last, is the poem. It is by Edward Thomas:

In Memoriam (Easter 1915)

The flowers left thick at nightfall in the wood
This Eastertide call into mind the men,
Now far from home, who, with their sweethearts, should
Have gathered them and will do never again.

I asked them to comment on the poem in writing, linking their remarks to parts of the poem. None of the children did this last part, except to identify the rhymes. Some of the children – about a third of them – were to a greater or lesser degree frustrated by the task, and not sympathetic to the poem: 'I don't like the poem because it sounds sad' wrote one. The class extrovert doodled on his copy: a spoiled ballot paper. Another comment was 'I don't like it, it's not fun'. This last is worrying. As I have written above, many children leaving primary schools, used to the popular diet of poetry that most publishers provide, would be forgiven for thinking that poetry exists to make one laugh. But one of the most negative notes ended: 'The poem made me think about the meaning'.

By now, for me, 'In Memoriam (Easter 1915)' was an even finer piece than I had thought it before. This was a result both of my composing the prose account, with the attendant business of paying the poem some real attention, and also of my several readings of the poem to the children and my discussion of it with them. What a fine teacher teaching is – for the teacher himself!

I asked the children some questions, but before I did so I felt that it was crucial to make it clear to them that this was not a test and that there were no right or wrong answers. I meant to ask the children to speak the poem aloud. To taste it, as Seamus Heaney says that we should. But I forgot. Teaching is a frenetic activity these days and one often forgets things. The questions asked were:

1. What is the poet saying?

2. How is he saying it?

3. Can you look at the rhyme?

4. And the alliteration?

5. Who do you think the men and their sweethearts are?

6. Where are the men going? Give reasons for your answer.

7. What is the mood of the poem? Say why you think it is what it is.

8. Do you like/dislike the poem? Say why.

I watched the children at work. Were they paying the poem the same sort of attention that I'd paid it? The atmosphere was tense. This was partly because the experience was unique for the children, partly because it was difficult and partly because the following week the children were to face their SATs.

The children who said that they did not like the poem often used the word 'confusing'. One child criticized it for being 'complicated'. Melissa wrote: 'It takes a while to catch on to what the writer is on about.' Francesca stated: 'I don't like it because its language is horrible because it has strange words in it and it took me ages to work out what it meant.' But she went on to write: 'The poet is saying it a bit like a riddle so that you can think about it and when you work it out you think about it even more.' Much as Edward Thomas (or almost any other poet) would dislike to be thought of as merely writing riddles, Francesca is homing in on something here. A poem does not offer itself up as immediately as other genres of writing. This was probably her first intimation of the presence of levels of ambiguity in a good poem.

Then came a lovely piece of learning and teaching. I like it especially because it arose out of a question from the children and confusion from the teacher and myself, and not from the conventionally expected ped-agogical confidence. Kirsty asked Lorna and I: 'What is it when you write something in a poem about some-thing, but you use something else?' Tentatively, we suggested similes and metaphors, but they were not the concepts Kirsty required. 'Write down what you are aiming at,' I said, and she wrote: 'The author is talking about a war but using flowers and people to explain it.' I thought of T. S. Eliot's objective correlative, 'a set of objects, a situation, a chain of events which shall be the formula of that particular emotion' (quoted in Gray, 1984). Of course, this does not apply exactly to Kirsty's writing here; but she has glimpsed the understand-ing that objects in poems – here the flowers and sweethearts – offer a way for poets to write about other things – in this case emotions connected with the war.

Jasmin, who tried 'ventured' in her composition, wrote about Thomas's: 'I don't know whether I like it, it's strange. On the other hand I sort of realised what he's on about.'

After a break, in spite of my misgivings about bio-graphical information in the close reading of poetry, I revealed something about Edward Thomas to the chil-dren. I told them that he had only been writing poems for about two years when he wrote this one; that it was about young men going to the front during the First World War; and that Thomas himself was killed by a shell at Arras the following year. Most modern critics probably deplore the use of such biographical material in the close analysis of a poem and, in part, I agree with them. The children would have disagreed: 'At first I didn't understand the poem and didn't like it, but when we were told what the poem meant I began to like it.'

None of the children picked up the significance of Easter until I dropped a few heavy hints.

The reader may well feel that I have offered the children a difficult poem. But I wouldn't have felt happy offering a poem, however good, by Causley for example, that did not present ambiguities. In any case, there is a tendency to offer children work that is not only too easy, but patronizing: children are capable of much more than many teachers assume. And officials – inspectors, politicians and the like – routinely under-rate what children are capable of.

If the Edward Thomas example is difficult, the next example is even more so. Here is another prose paraphrase. Once again, I hope my readers will try to make it into a piece of concise verse:

Two seasons to an infant

Little girl, are you worrying about death
About this place and the green shapes falling from
*   the tree?*
Those things, just as everything mankind had
*   made, you*
With your new mental processes, you worry
*   about, do you?*
Ah! as the inner part of you loses its youth
It won't worry so much about such views

Soon, nor breathe sadly and deeply
Though planets of sad-timber green-food lie;
But you will shed tears and understand the
*   question.*
At this moment, don't worry, girl, about what you
*   or it are called.*
Sadness's bubblings of water [or Aprils] are
*   identical.*
No speaking organ, no thinking organ put out into
*   public*
What the inner organ listened to, phantom made
*   chance thoughts:*
It is the plant injury, or disease, humankind was
*   created for,*
It is you, named little girl, you are sad for the
*   loss of.*

What did Dawn make of this? She attempted a poem
derived from my prose. Here are the notes she made
before she gave up:

Is this your beginning (name – Hannah?)
Do you fear the end?
Does this world
Of trees and swirling leaves
Unsettle [deleted] disturb your untainted
*   thoughts?*
In time your soul will ease
And (though you may weep) – illusion
                                        loss
                                        meaninglessness
you will grow wise
for now, rest easy in innocence

tears and rain are one –
words cannot reveal your soul
only the world's.

She stopped, understandably, at the phrase 'sad-timer green-food'. But despite this, I still felt the paraphrase was worth offering to children.

Here are some juniors working with the same text. They are 11-year-old members of a 'Gifted and Talented' group in an 'Education Action Zone' in the east of England. No doubt my readers will be able to break this code: the children had been identified as potentially more clever and fluent writers than both others in their year group, and than their environment allowed them to be. The adviser, who had invited me to work with the children, had told me that they, like many of the children in this area, lacked 'self-esteem'. Indeed, pupils from local comprehensives, with whom I had worked the previous year, had frequently, and very worryingly, described their attempts at poetry as 'rubbish' and 'crap'.

These top juniors were not as negative. They had been brought together from four schools, and worked in pairs on the prose paraphrase. Here are two examples of the result:

Anne, troubled by death you should not be
Earth and leaves dissolving
Something men have made.
Your new thoughts and actions bother you, they
*   shouldn't*
As physically you have progressed
You won't fret at those views.

Soon no breath will overcome you.
Though earths of upset wool-coloured nutrients lie
But you will cry and comprehend the problem
Right now don't fret about names.
Springs are the same.
No vocal chords or brain are to be put in public.
What the heart heard demons made chance ideas
It is the pains, or illnesses man was made for
It is you, Anne, you are upset for the loss of.
(Lindsay and Louise, both aged 11)

Little one, worried about death
And the green leaves falling from the great oak
  trees?
Things mankind had made you
With your dreaming worry, do you not?
The humorous part of you loses youth
It won't worry much about views
Not breathe sadly, deeply
Though planets of tearful logs spinach lie
You shed tears and understand questions
Now, don't worry about what you or it are called.
Showers of water are similar
Speaking organ, thinking organ, put out
The inner organ listened to phantom made
  thoughts.
It is plant injury, disease mankind has created.
It is you, little one, you are sad for the loss of.
(Danielle, aged 10)

'[W]ool-coloured nutrients'; 'tearful logs spinach': these are attempts at the phrase Dawn balked at, which I had given as 'sad-timber green-food'. Other children wrote 'crying wood vegetables', 'weeping-wood blue nut', 'sorrowed bark' and 'unhappy-wood mouldy meals'. The last got very close to the original (see below). But look at these beautiful last lines: 'It is you, Anne, you are upset for the loss of'; 'It is you, little one, you are sad for the loss of . . .'.

Eventually, the children saw the lovely Gerard Manley Hopkins on which the paraphrase was based:

Spring and Fall: to a young child

Margaret, are you grieving
Over Goldengrove unleaving?
Leaves, like the things of man, you
With your fresh thoughts care for, can you?
Ah! as the heart grows older
It will come to such sights colder
By and by, nor spare a sigh
Though worlds of wanwood leafmeal lie;
And yet you will weep and know why.
Now no matter, child, the name:
Sorrow's springs are the same.
Nor mouth had, no nor mind, expressed
What heart heard of, ghost guessed:
It is the blight man was born for,
It is Margaret you mourn for.

'Wanwood leafmeal' – ah, of course!

'Why do teachers tacitly reject the idea that a child might think of something that is beyond them.

3
Children Writing Poetry

My candle is my Way finder
And my Light bearer

(Oliver)

Mia fratelo vedera dal cielo?
(Can my brother see me from Heaven?)

(Martina)

The word 'creativity' presents at least two problems. First, it is unfashionable in our education system, partly because its protean nature makes it both difficult to define and immeasurable. It is not subject to the habit of unremitting testing. This immeasurability makes it so exciting for the creative, and so frustrating for the uncreative.

Second, creativity is associated with a movement in the sixties and seventies that I have described in my introduction. Some of the adherents of this movement were less concerned with making art than with the dubious business of self-expression. This had two effects. It led to sentimental outpourings, and to a neglect of form – and form, or structure, is essential to creativity. All this blackened the reputation of creativity as a force in the classroom.

Take structure. Ask anyone to write a poem, or a story, about his or her childhood, and he or she will,

justifiably, look blank. But give that person a structure –
'Look through this photograph album and write a
couplet about each picture', for example, or 'write a
haiku about each house you have lived in, or each
school you have attended', and it becomes easier. Art
does not require license to gush, to pour out; on the
contrary, it requires containment.

Sometimes, however, when we give children a
structure that a poet has invented, there is another
problem: the poems the children write are too close
to the original. They cannot break free from the teaching involved, neither the teacher's teaching, nor (more
importantly) the poem's teaching, and anyone who is
familiar with poetry recognizes the model that the
children have used. This would be inadmissible in a
professional poet, unless he or she were writing a
parody, a pastiche or a homage.

The way around this is a teacher's way: the poem
may look familiar, but can we identify learning going
on? If so, we can justify the child's imitation of a
Shakespeare speech, or a traditional rhyme, or a
poem by a contemporary writer like John Gohorry.
Indeed, that learning is an element in the child's
creativity. The originality is not in the poem, but in the
learning.

I want to define creativity, for the sake of this book,
as *the use of poetic devices in the making of original
verbal artefacts within structures*. I know how inelegant
this sounds, but that definition contains critical terms in
it that I can't do without. Perhaps surprisingly, 'poetic'
is not one of these. That word has become so debased
in normal discourse that it can now mean 'precious',
'irrelevant to life', or even, if you trained as a teacher at

a rugby college, 'unmanly'. The critical terms are 'original' and 'structures'. By 'poetic devices', I mean (especially but not exclusively) simile, metaphor, rhyme and rhythm.

Simile acts like a structure. To involve the word 'like' makes you contain the feeling, the impression, the idea, or whatever it is, within a cage. When I search in my mind for examples of creativity, I recall describing to my friend Peter Dixon an occasion when I was with children in a Yorkshire dale listening to a thrush singing. I asked the children to make up a sentence saying what the sound was 'like', what it 'resembled', what it 're-minded them of'. After much dross which I have for-gotten ('tweeting' and 'twittering', 'singly sweetly' and other dead phrases were in there, you can be sure), a girl said that it was 'like a ring being dropped and then being picked up again'.

I asked her to repeat her phrase. I listened carefully, and asked the other children, and the teacher, to listen carefully, too. 'Like a ring being dropped and then being picked up again.' I knew that this was good and I was especially pleased that I did not totally understand (and I still do not) what she meant. I can hear, in birdsong, the ring being dropped – and it is brilliant – but being picked up again? I can glimpse that, but only just. But poetry is obscure sometimes. Why do teachers tacitly reject the idea that a child might think of something that is beyond them?

Peter then told me he had been teaching a class in Newcastle, and had asked them about gold. 'As gold as –?' he prompted. 'Yellow paint?' came one answer. 'No'. 'As a gold ring?' came another. 'No,' said Peter. And then a boy said in a Geordie accent (I wish you could hear Peter's version of it): 'As gold as a glass of Newcastle beer.'

That's creativity. We are looking for sentences that have never been uttered before, and here are two: 'The birdsong sounds like a ring being dropped and then being picked up again'; and something – a field of corn, perhaps? – was 'As gold as a glass of Newcastle beer'. While both little pieces of creativity are imprisoned in simile, they are not imprisoned in a teacher's limited expectations. In his lovely book *The Silver Toilet Roll* (1979), Dixon makes it clear that if a child finds something to do with the inside of a toilet roll that is new, that is creativity. But if the child follows the instructions of a teacher to make a Father Christmas, identical to the Father Christmases of his or her classmates, that is not creativity. He makes the point with telling irony:

HOME WORK FOR THE TEACHER Sit down and copy out one of Dickens' novels ... DON'T TRY to write your own, you might get it wrong.

(Dixon, 1979)

There has been debate for years about whether children can write poetry at all. The poet Vernon Scannell is scathingly insistent that they cannot (for his remarks on this subject, see my book, 1997); but, as Tunnicliffe says, quoting Auden, 'we are all image-makers, or "proto-poets"'. Children, in my experience, are stronger proto-poets than almost anyone over the age of puberty. The only older people who are better at poetry are those who combine wider experience, intensive reading and practice of poetry, with a retention of

'Children, in my experience, are stronger proto-poets than almost anyone over the age of puberty.'

certain aspects of childhood: a sense of curiosity and wonder, a dread of getting things wrong.

I have always, like Dylan Thomas (see the beginning of his *Collected Poems*, 1957), linked creativity with religion and, especially, with the first chapter of Genesis and the first few verses of Chapter 2: 'And God saw everything that he had made, and, behold, it was very good' (1:31). Sometimes I read the Genesis passage to children, and suggest that by the end of the day they will have written something – a first draft, only – that they will be able to stand back from. And they will be able to say about it, like God looking at his new world: 'That's good.'

Recently, I have been using poetry, especially poetry from the past, as a stimulus to help children to write. This serves two purposes: it introduces children to poetry and it helps them to write. First, I concentrated on Shakespeare (Sedgwick, 1999a). Later, I used poems by the Hebrew psalmists, and the Hebrew authors of Genesis (as translated in the King James Version). I used work by Geoffrey Chaucer, William Blake, John Clare, Thomas Hood, Christina Rossetti, Wilfred Owen, Gerard Manley Hopkins and Edward Thomas, among others (Sedgwick, 2000a, 2001). In this book, I have used poems by a modern poet, John Gohorry, Saxon kennings, Anon, as well as a fragment from Thomas Lovell Beddoes, and Hopkins and Edward Thomas again.

High Places

Here are some children writing creatively with the help of John Gohorry. First, his poem:

High Places
I love high places
– the top of the hill
where the wind races
and birds come to fill

their hearts with delight
at the blue distance
their songs must aim at.
All round, the immense

sky reaches and spins;
cloud shifts and dissolves
as it imagines
shapes for cloud puzzles,

while my heart resolves
its griefs and desires
in the perspectives
of the hill's pleasures.

Then let me climb high
to where I belong;
this hill-top, where I
am cloud, space, birdsong.

When there was no-one else in, I practised reading this at home. This poem, like all poems, requires practice, especially in the long sentence from 'All round' to 'pleasures', which requires good breathing and an understanding, or at least an intuition, of what is happening syntactically: two main clauses, and two subordinate ones. Often teachers' readings of poems betray a lack of interest in such things. In fact, they sometimes betray a lack of any interest in the poem at all. I also noted the rhymes in the poem, of which more later. I found that this preparatory study was educational: to look at how a poem was constructed was learning for me, as well as a necessary component of my teaching. And he or she who teaches without learning him or herself is not teaching at all, but training.

In the classroom, I read it to the children with as much care as I could. I pointed out afterwards how it starts simply, with a four-word clause/line – 'I love high places' – and then immediately becomes more complex. That complexity grows until the beginning of the last stanza. The poem then becomes simple again: 'Then let me climb high.' I pointed out how short the lines were ('Poets are paid by the line!'). I explained, as best I could, some difficult words: 'dissolves', 'resolves' and 'perspectives'.

There are, of course, other ways of helping children to write poetry in lines, including counting syllables, and writing initially in prose form, then putting slashes (/) where you breathe as you read it again. This latter method is probably the most, you might say, 'organic' way of doing this. You could teach children to hear beats, and ask them to write in two-beat or three-beat lines. But artificial ways, like counting syllables – and like talking about payment – can also work.

I talked about the rhyme. There are, I pointed out, only four full rhymes: 'places / races', 'hill / fill', 'high / I' and 'belong / bird song'. Significantly, these rhymes come at points in the poem that are relatively simple. The other rhymes are all half, or pararhymes: 'delight / at', 'distance / immense', 'spins / imagines', 'dissolves / puzzles', 'resolves / perspectives' and 'desires / perspectives'. I asked the children not to use rhyme at all.

I said that I loved 'muddy places / where the brown wet earth / pulls at my boots' and 'sunny places / seen from the tops / of aeroplane steps', and 'silent places / on Sunday mornings / when my son is still asleep / and my wife / has gone for a swim . . .'. I emphasized those possible line breaks with long pauses, and with hand gestures.

I collected some adjectives from the children. What places do you like? I was offered 'cold', 'snowy', 'ghostly', 'loud', 'quiet', 'dreamy', 'hot', 'cold', 'wet', 'seaside', 'busy', 'noisy' and 'musical' among many others. Ruhi offered no adjectives at all, and was silent during this lighting-up session. It was fascinating to watch how the children's choice of places exposed their personalities. The teacher affectionately nodded her head when a boisterous person said 'I love noisy places', or a quiet one said 'I love silent places', or a horse-riding child said 'I love horsey places'. Poetry drives to the centre of things. It was silently driving Ruhi.

I then asked the children to make up, in their minds, a second line beginning with 'where'. Someone offered 'I love silent places / where I can be myself . . .', I insisted that he go on: 'And . . . ? What's it like?' He added 'and no-one gets in my way.'

I wrote my own draft. It is important, sometimes, to write alongside the children for two reasons. First, it impresses on them that writing is not only something you have to do in school when you are a child, or when you are a famous writer like Ted Hughes or Roald Dahl. Second, it teaches the children not to make a priority of mechanical problems like spelling and so on: they cannot come up for that kind of help because the teacher is writing him or herself, and must not be interrupted.

I often 'magically' change the classroom with a clap of my hands into 'a study where 30 poets are writing – it must be a silent place where there is no unnecessary noise'. This may be a trick, but it seems to me to be a practical way of getting the kind of silence that work of this kind requires. It is much better than simply demanding hush with persistent shushing and half-angry barks and nagging.

In the silence, we wrote. My draft read:

I love clouds
I would love to be like Constable
And make studies of them.
That cloud that is 'like a camel' indeed
Or a weasel or a whale.

I study the words:
Cumulus, heaped and piled,
Cirrus, a tufted filament;
And stratus, laid down; like a field of snow;
And nimbus, a god's splendour.

I look up:
A confused flag
Like humanity
The way flags are not
A leaden grey

A bright silver
Tinged with the gold
Of a hidden sun
White wisps sailing
Into a blue unknown.

Then I reworked it at home:

Clouds

I would like to be like Constable
and make studies of them. The way
they're like language, changing
but not suddenly; and something
for all of us to own.

I love the words:
cumulus, heaped and piled,
cirrus, a tufted filament;
stratus, laid down like a field of snow;
nimbus, a god's splendour.

Look up, and look until it hurts
at the million-patterned flag
in the sky, this morning
a bright silver
tinged with the gold
of a hidden sun.

Eventually, long after my visit to the school, I reworked my version in a syllabic count:

Clouds

I'd like to be
John Constable
and make studies of them. The way
they're like language, changing but not
suddenly; the way they're something
all of us own.

I love the words:
cumulus, heaped,
piled; cirrus, tufted filament;
stratus, laid down like a field
of snow; nimbus, a pagan
godling's splendour.

Look up, and look
until it hurts
at the million-patterned flag.
Yesterday, grey. Today it's a
bright silver, tinged with the gold
of a hidden sun.

I kept all this to myself. I should have shared it with the children. Among them, without benefit of second or third drafts, the silent Ruhi took my breath away with the following:

I love worship places
where the holy pages
touch the tips of my fingers
and prayers are being spoken
by the soft voices.
I love worship places
where the Azan has been called

and men get ready to pray
on the patterned carpet.
I love worship places
where I can face the kaba
and pray with the Imam
with sisters
shoulder to shoulder.
I love worship places
where people say
peace be upon you,
and hug you
for respect.

Pax vobiscum, Ruhi.

'High Places' is not an easy poem. But we should not be afraid of difficulty in poems for children. It is insulting to present them with poems that we conceive of as easy, in that dreary phrase, 'at their level'. Are they all at the same level as each other? Is each of them at the same level at the same time? What is a level? How would I feel about anyone speculating about the level I was on? Offering most children Eliot's *Four Quartets* would be absurd, although some children would find things to enjoy in it. Teaching is a question of finding something that has some relation to what the children already know, but which extends them into realms that they do not know. Gohorry's poem is an example of this match being made perfectly.

'One way of looking at it', writes Matthew Sweeney in his introduction to *The New Faber Book of Children's Verse* (quoted in Mole, 2002), 'is that a good children's poem is two poems simultaneously – one for children, one for adults.' Certainly, a poem that only works for children – or for children as seen by a certain sort of adult – is a dire thing. Here is an example:

> *Thank you, pretty cow, that made*
> *Pleasant milk, to soak my bread;*
> *Every day, and every night,*
> *Warm, and fresh, and sweet, and white...*

That verse comes from Opie and Opie (1973) and is by Ann and Jane Taylor. Of course, we view children differently now, and we do not expect them to think like this. Our children's experience of milk (and of almost everything else) is different from the child contemporaries of the poets. But it is bad (and was bad then) because it is inconceivable as a poem written for adults. It is worth examining much modern verse for children in the light of this criterion. Charles Causley has said that he does not know, when he begins to write a poem, whether it will be for adults or for children. I find that few of his poems for children are not also poems for adults.

'Oh what if the fowler'

John Mole has highlighted (2002) a poem that modern children cannot be expected to understand but which, nevertheless, entrances them. I have to say that I cannot fully understand it either: and that is, partly, the point. Everyone can see what 'Thank you, pretty cow, that made...' is about; much as everyone can see the point of some doggerel from a comedian. But poetry only comes into being when there is ambiguity.

W. H. Auden and John Garrett collected this strange poem as long ago as 1935:

> O what if the fowler my blackbird has taken?
>   The roses of dawn blossom over the sea;
> Awaken, my blackbird, awaken, awaken,
>   And sing to me out of red fuchsia tree!
>
> O what if the fowler my blackbird has taken?
>   The sun lifts its head from the lap of the sea –
> Awaken, my blackbird, awaken, awaken,
>   And sing to me out of red fuchsia tree!
>
> O what if the fowler my blackbird has taken?
>   The mountain grows white with the birds of the
>   sea;
> But down in my garden forsaken, forsaken,
>   I'll weep all the day by my red fuchsia tree!
>   (Charles Dalmon)

Now, when a teacher asked me to work on parodies with her class, I was not sure. After all, a parody (from the Greek for 'mock poem') has ridicule as one of its central features. How, I wondered, were children to mock a poem that they had only just encountered? Was the idea ethically justifiable anyway, given that one duty of the teacher of literature is to introduce children to good poetry, and to teach respect for it? And is parody not an essentially adult form? You have, after all, to know a poem intimately in order to take the rise out of it. You get to know a poem well; you love it; *then* you can mock it, much as you can laugh at the idiosyncrasies of someone you love. I anticipated that the children would not write parodies at all but, what the French call *hommages*, tributes to the original.

I handed out copies of the original. The children read it aloud, first individually, and then in groups. Afterwards, I read the poem to the children. I suggested that the first line could be changed in various ways. The first noun, 'fowler', could be changed into any noun denoting a person that had two syllables. The children suggested 'butcher', 'baker' and 'teacher' among others. Later came 'mother' and 'father'. The children worked in pairs, and this poem arrived:

O what if the diver my dolphin has taken?
  The stars of twilight shine over the earth.
Be here my dolphin, oh, be here, oh be here
  And call to me soon at the time of your birth.

O what if the diver my dolphin has taken?
  The moon floats gently, it's lighting the earth.
Be here my dolphin, oh, be here, oh be here
  And call to me soon at the time of your birth.

O what if the diver my dolphin has taken?
  The waves grow huge, as huge as a life.
And lying on top of the great open sea
  I cry at the death (oh so soon) of her birth.
                    (Amy, aged 11, and Alice, aged 8)

These girls had picked up the alliteration in the Dalmon poem and the way it suggests the direction the poem is going to take. They also took on the rhyme, very well. Even the false half-rhyme 'life / birth' does its job. I had more to do with the final version of this piece than usual. The diction is all from the girls, but they were a foot short in lines 4, 7 and 12, and I suggested the repetition of an iambic phrase ('be here') and the use of an anapaest, ('oh so soon'). I explained these terms by tapping on my palms. Justifying myself I would say that the conversation we had about these additions was educational in that it taught the girls something about rhythm, both technically and in terms of the feel of the poem. Looking back now, I wish I had set the children the task of finding the right feet themselves.

Here is another poem:

Oh what if the vet has stolen my dog.
Left behind on the peg is his lead.
Come back, my dog, come back come back
And bark to me under the shady apple tree.

Oh what if the vet has stolen my dog.
The clouds lift him up from the great world below.
Come back, my dog, come back come back
And bark to me under the shady apple tree.

Oh what if the vet has stolen my dog.
The basket is left empty and cold.
I'll cry and cry until you come
Back to my shady apple tree.
(Sophie, aged 10, and Isobel, aged 9)

The poem is about Sophie's dog. Her smiling mother told me later, when I met her in the street: 'That poem made me cry . . . Our dog was run over a while ago.' My request that the children should write a parody had led these two girls into making a piece with genuine feeling. They were learning about language, of course; but they were also learning about deep emotions, in this case about recent feelings of great sadness.

The candle

I wrote about the candle poem from Alec Clegg's book *The Excitement of Writing* (1965: introduction), and I wondered then if the poem would have been even better if it had been taught with another poem. I read that poem to children, and I read a rough kenning of my own. I am not proud of it, and did no further work: I merely used it as a teaching tool about kennings:

From my study window

A rescue-beetle buzzes
against the mix of rain-bags
and the heaven's ceiling.
Message-lines radiate
from the tops of poles.
My people-carrier waits
against the road's edge
as a child-bearer hassles
her children to the learning-house.
A honey-maker settles
for a moment
on my desk; explores with all
her precious five my word-makers.

I read this once, then I read the kennings in reverse order: 'word-makers', 'honey-maker', 'learning-house', 'child-bearer', 'people-carrier', 'message lines', 'heaven's ceiling', 'rain-bags' and 'rescue-beetle'. I chose reverse order because I thought that 'rescue-beetle' would be the most difficult. I live near a seaside hospital, where a helicopter is often required. One child got this reference immediately and it presented no problem at all to the rest. I then asked the children to write a list of kennings about a candle.

I had set two large candles up in the room; one group gathered round one, and the other around the second. I asked them to look at them more closely in turns. Then they wrote their own lists of kennings. Alex, for example, wrote:

Liquid maker
Darkness destroyer
Light bringer
Shape moulder
Body burner
Reservoir maker
Heat happener
Smooth cylinder
Body warmer
Non-electrical light

I asked the children to make his list of kennings into a poem. Alex wrote:

The shape moulder moulds
The light bringer brings
But only the brave go near the frightful body burner
The reservoir former forms
The liquid maker makes
But only the brave go near the frightful body burner

It's non-electrical light
It's a smooth cylinder
But only the brave go near the frightful body burner

I had not suggested that the children use repetition: Alex had decided this for himself.

I taught the lesson with more skill in another school. The children were younger – a range of Key Stage 2 plus some only just seven-year-olds – and I talked less, and let the children talk, and look, and smell, more. I would not have dreamed of teaching this lesson to them had I not succeeded (as I saw it) the day before with Year 6.

Eventually, Oliver took my breath away. While other children had been coming up with their sheets of paper asking: 'Is this all right?' and 'How do you spell ... ?' he had sat in front of me, ignoring my presence, studiously writing. This is what I saw when he finally agreed that I could see his work. Here is Oliver's first draft:

Way finder
Light bearer
Path to God
Light maker
Wax burner
Bird of light
Feather of fire
Night lighter
Fire dancer
Dancing flame
Torch of freedom
Darkness fighter
Light of the world

Light of the room
Animal of fire
Lighting darkness
Fire tongue
Messenger to God
Path to freedom

The teachers shook their heads, impressed, although later they told me that Oliver was always 'good with words'. I thought: 'I wish I could write like that.' The freedom of it! Oliver and I went into a nearby class-room, where there was a computer already set up with a word processing programme and a printer, and I asked him to add 'the mortar to your bricks...the flesh to your skeleton'. (I had already explained this idea to all the children.) I also suggested that Oliver might change the order of some of his kennings as he redrafted on the computer.

He came up with this, with some word-processing help from me:

My candle is my Way finder
And my Light bearer
My flame is my Path to God
And a Light maker
It is my Wax burner
And my Bird of light
It is my Feather of fire
My Night dancer
It is a Dancing flame
My Torch of freedom
It is a Darkness fighter
And the Lighter of the world

It is my Light of the room
My Animal of fire
It is Lighting darkness
And a Fire tongue
It is the Messenger to God
And the Path to freedom.

The youngest child in the group wrote this next poem. I had held one of the candles – a tall white one – high in my hands, and walked solemnly around the room with it, as though I were a priest, or a crucifer:

The prececien [procession] wax stick
leads us through
the dark back to
god where it is safe.

The waving flame
shows us the
way to the path
  of kindness.

The fire holder shows us
the way to
the safest place of all.

The burning fire
scares bad spirits and
ghosts away.

The wax stick
holds the flame and
the flame scares the
bad spirits.

The waving flame
scares some people
away and attacks the
   night.
The night frightener
scares ghosts away.

(Megan, aged 6)

Drafting often presents a problem both for teachers and children. In the 1980s, this activity was less understood in English education than it is now. These days, it is recognized that it is simply pointless to teach poetry without an emphasis on the work that the writer has to go through; the crossings out, the arrows leading from the first text to possible additions, the new sheets of paper and the writing-outs. In this lesson, it was painless: the first draft was the list of kennings that each child wrote, and the second draft was the kennings with words that linked them.

I saw a peacock

Another idea comes from Brownjohn (1989):

I saw a Peacock with a fiery tail,
I saw a blazing Comet drop down hail,
I saw a Cloud with ivy circled round,
I saw a sturdy Oak creep on the ground,
I saw a Pismire swallow up a whale,
I saw a raging sea brimful of ale,
I saw a Venice Glass sixteen foot deep,
I saw a Well full of men's tears that weep,

> *I saw their Eyes all in a flame of fire,*
> *I saw a House big as the moon and higher,*
> *I saw the Sun even in the midst of night,*
> *I saw the Man that saw this wondrous sight.*
> (Collected in Sedgwick, 2002a)

Brownjohn would not, she says, make 'too many claims for this poem'. I think she sells it short. Anyway, I followed her advice in teaching this poem: the children began by writing a line that makes sense and setting it out like this:

playing on her recorder

I saw my sister

Then the child writes a second line, and slots it in like this:

playing on her recorder

I saw my sister   *breathing fire*
I saw a dragon

And so on. The children were very amused by the odd effect of the half-lines colliding. Here are a couple of the completed poems:

I saw a dog playing	*on her recorder*
I saw my sister	*breathing fire*
I saw a dragon	*writing a song*
I saw a musician	*roar with anger*
I saw a lion	*squeak with fear*
I saw a mouse	*rumble fearlessly*
I saw a storm	*squeal across the floor*

I saw a chair   *whisper in the wind*
I saw the trees   *prancing about*
I saw a dancer   *trumpet noisily*
I saw an elephant   *being drawn back*
I saw my curtains   *fly on her broomstick*
I saw a witch   *as beautiful as can be*
I saw the new day   *growl ferociously*
And I saw the year   *in which all these things*
                     occurred
                     (Alexandra, aged 10)

I saw a wimp gallant and bold
I saw a knight twist and curl
I saw a whirlpool screeching and squawking
I saw a raven squiggle and squirm
I saw a worm hunting his prey
I saw a lion playing his tricks
I saw a pixie charging and snorting
I saw a bull run for a medal
I saw an athlete crackle and spit
I saw a fire open its pages
I saw a book painting a picture
I saw Picasso rolling around
I saw the eye that saw these things!
                     (Jerem, aged 10)

The strong verbs in this writing are striking: 'twist', 'curl', 'squiggle', 'squirm', 'crackle' and 'spit'. The poem would have been even more striking if the present participles ('screeching', 'squawking', 'painting', 'rolling', etc.) had been main verbs: 'screech', 'squawk', 'paint', 'roll'.

In another school, I introduced rhyme:

I saw a skeleton playing in a band
I saw a boy sinking in the sand
I saw a crab shooting up to space
I saw a firework with a painted face
I saw a girl ticking back time
I saw a clock that tasted like lime
I saw a lemon soaring through a cloud
I saw a plane playing very loud
I saw a drummer eating bamboo
I saw a panda with a pot of glue
I saw a carpenter give someone an awful fright
I saw the man who saw this wondrous sight
(Lydia, aged 10)

'A river curled and asleep'

I found a short poem in Keegan (2000). It is by Thomas Lovell Beddoes, of whom I know nothing except what is offered by Benet (1973): 'an eccentric, melancholy man with a taste for the macabre [who] wrote in the tradition of the Elizabethan poetic drama...a great admirer of Shelley...'. The poem reads:

A Lake

A lake
Is a river curled and asleep like a snake.

It uses, in its eleven words, a metaphor and a simile, two of the central components of poetry. 'Metaphor' comes from the Greek 'to carry over'; it is the description of one thing in terms of another. A simile (as Davies says) 'makes the comparison more explicit ... by using the words "like" or "as".' Here Beddoes describes a lake in terms of a river, then adds an animal in his simile.

I wrote the poem on the whiteboard, without any teaching – I had to go to another class. Later the teacher presented me with these results. Some of these poems are sentimental. Some are strange and difficult for the adult's eye to see. But all of them show children playing creatively with language:

A puddle
Is water when God had just let out his bath.

(Anon.)

A tree
Is a frog made up of toads as well.

(Anon.)

A wave
Is a dolphin diving into the water.

(Ross)

A wave
Is a herd of unicorns rushing in the sea.

(Bethany)

A raindrop
Is a tiny tear as if someone in heaven is crying.

(Sarah)

'Some are strange and difficult for the adult's eye to see. But all of them show children playing creatively with language.

*A rose
Is a spiky sea urchin opening itself.*

(John)

Later I taught the same poem in another school, pointing out the alliteration, the rhyme and the simile in the Beddoes poem (I do not usually teach rhyme). Amy's first draft was:

*A cloud
Is a fine field in the morning, it looks like God
has it ploughed.*

She had attempted a rhyme, 'cloud / ploughed'.

Before she wrote her second draft, Amy asked me: 'What is that cloud that looks flat?' There was some debate about this between the teacher and myself. Resort to the dictionary lead to this:

*A cirrus cloud
Is a fine field at dawn horse-ploughed.*

In her second draft, the rhyme stays the same, but has more point. 'God' has gone. The horse has arrived. And, although she insisted on pronouncing 'cirrus' as 'cirrius' when she read it aloud to the class, Amy has written a poem.

A final word

Martina wrote this next poem. I had asked her, and her classmates, to write a list of questions they'd love to

93

know the answers to, but did not think they ever would.
I had suggested that this would make a 'philosophical
poem'. She started hers in her first language, Italian,
and then, at my request, put it into her second language, English:

Cuando muoero?
Cuand la mia famiglia muorera?
Ci stara mai paco dostrco al mondo?
Cuande novole ci stano?
Cuande alber ci stano?
Il mare cuand e grande?
One sucedera sevodo in cielo?
Mia fratelo vedera dal cielo?

When will I die?
When will my family die?
Will there be peace in the world?
How many skies are there?
How many trees are there?
How long is the sea?
What will happen if I go to heaven?
Can my brother see me from heaven?

Afterword

In the beginning was the word

Why is poetry important? This is an urgent question at a difficult time for anyone concerned with creativity in education. The materialism of our system; its emphasis on what pays rather than what teaches; its managerialism, that looks at children in terms of what they must become, rather than what they are – all this is profoundly anti-poetic and, therefore, anti-creative. When poetry is considered officially in the National Literacy Strategy, it is reduced to little machines like limericks, thin poems and calligrams. It is nothing to do with the creative tussle between the form and feeling that is real poetry.

If we want to know why poetry is important we have to ask first why language is important. Language is the single most important possession of the human race. It is, says Coleridge, '. . . the armoury of the human mind, and at once contains the trophies of the past, and the weapons of its future, conquests' (quoted in Trench, 1908). Many other human things matter to us, of course. Some are even central to our very existence: being healthy, or falling in love, or believing or not believing in God. In the curriculum, you could make a case for dance or drama being at the very heart of the matter. Scientists and mathematicians would make an altogether different case.

All these have language as a *sine qua non*. To be what we are when we run or dance, when we express our deepest emotions (and our shallowest), when we worship or deny the relevance of worship, when we calculate and measure, is to use language. Conventionally, we believe that language is there to express our thinking. We believe that 'Language is the amber in which a thousand and one precious thoughts have been safely embedded and preserved' (Trench, 1908). Although there is some truth in this, it sells language short. It is horribly static: 'embedded', 'preserved'. This is like believing that we learn something, and then use language – speech or writing – merely to reinforce or to contain that learning. But to view language as fossilized in that beautiful resin, irretrievably still, stagnant even, is a notion that, as soon as I reflect on it (with my language, of course) fills me with disquiet.

We could not think were it not for language. Some people insist that they think in pictorial or (less often) musical images. But whenever I ask a new friend who is using English as a second or third language, 'Do you think in English or Swedish?', that person never says to me, 'I think in neither, I think in pictures,' or 'I think in music.' Sometimes they say, 'I think in English when I am talking to you, but at home, I think in Swedish.' As a lousy French speaker (*'une bière s'il vous plaît'*) and a pathetic Spanish one (*una cerveza por favor*), I know I am thinking in English when I try to speak French or Spanish. Either way, even as I have an image of a glass of beer in my head, I am thinking in a language.

If we cannot think without language, we cannot live without it either. Language-less, we die. Roland Barthes (1982) writes 'Any refusal of language is a death.' Reflecting on this, I thought how a fraught silence in a close relationship is a little death, and how a refusal to negotiate by one of two warring partners leads to many deaths.

If we look seriously at the curriculum, we see that we cannot teach any subject without also teaching language. A PE class (traditionally seen by many arts education students as a low-status lesson) is, among other things, a lesson in language and a powerful one. It teaches children about the importance of listening and about ways of listening: it teaches them more about speech as we ask them to interpret in words what we are asking them to do in movement. Music, of course, offers a seductive alternative to language, as does painting. Practitioners of these arts often suggest that they have a way of learning, a way of thinking, that does not involve language. But their communication is less subtle than the communication that language enables and, in any case, it always, at least ultimately, involves language. Language can try to interpret painting and music: hence the number of radio programmes devoted to doing just that. The notion of painting and music trying to interpret language is absurd.

Music is incapable of precision. I have just listened, once again, to the whole of Tchaikowsky's *First Piano Concerto*, paying it more attention than I did in my youth. It communicated much about feeling. But it was neither capable of argument, nor of making me feel the intricacies of feeling. Without language, it couldn't have been written. There may be thoughts

97

that lie too deep for tears, but there are no thoughts that lie too deep for language.

Language makes us human or, more accurately, is the prerequisite for our humanity. In his beautiful poem 'Their Lonely Betters', Auden (1976) writes, as he sits in his beach-chair listening to the noises of the birds in his garden, 'Not one of them was capable of lying / There was not one which knew that it was dying.' The birds were merely following instincts. We humans, on the other hand, as we understand to our cost, can lie, and be lied to; and we know that we, and everyone else around us, is dying. 'Words', Auden concludes, 'are for those with promises to keep.' And that is the speaking, writing, listening *human* race. You could sum up language's centrality by quoting the first verse of St John's Gospel: 'In the beginning was the word . . .'.

Emerson turns the corner with us from language to poetry when he writes 'Language is fossil poetry': 'The etymologist finds the deadest word to have been once a brilliant picture.' Every cliché was once a poetic usage. If we could hear, for example, the first human being saying that something – a disease, a rumour – 'spread like wildfire' we can glimpse what Emerson means. It must have been an intense moment for a speaker, assuming that his or her listeners had the time to listen to what he was saying, and that they weren't running away from something – a wildfire! – coming, flaming, towards them.

You can play the game with another cliché: to describe himself as being 'over the moon' with joy must have given a massive lift to someone's descriptions of their feelings. I imagine that person looking into the night, freshened with wonderful news. Now a football manager using that phrase is tiresome; and it makes it no less tiresome when he acknowledges beforehand that 'This may be a cliché, but...'. Christopher Ricks, quoted in Fowler (1996) wrote that 'A cliché begins as heartfelt, and then its heart sinks.' Every cliché was heartfelt once, and it was a pebble of poetry.

Today, in the United Kingdom, the cliché of the test, of measurement of the immeasurable, matters more than the grubby, glorious reality of education. Therefore, schools rise or fall on the basis of results, and the arts (grubby and glorious, if nothing else) have been pushed to one side, like discarded props from a school Shakespeare production. When I teach INSET courses on poetry, people say things like 'It was wonderful when we had time to work in this way', and 'I find I can't teach poetry now with the pressure of the SATs.' This is a dangerous state of affairs; poetry teaches so much. It is language at its most intense.

If you work on Thomas Hardy's poem 'Neutral Tones', or Gerard Manley Hopkins's poem, you will see what I mean. We come out of the experience of reading, writing and responding in this way with more understanding about language, about the situation described in the poem and about similar experiences in our own lives. We may not come out of it as happier or morally improved people, but we do come out of it as more human. Similarly, the children working with Edward Thomas's 'In Memoriam' gained an inkling of empathy with a country at war. This was just as important as a gathering of the historical facts. We can see poetic teaching at its most powerful, I think, when a committed teacher (committed to the poem, committed to the class, committed to the wonderful business of being a teacher) teaches a good poem. It is not only the pupil who learns, it is also the teacher.

Without poetry, it becomes more and more difficult to question what the important people think. Poetry's insistence on the danger of cliché is an attack on what has gone before. When poetry is suppressed in favour of an intimate knowledge of phonemes, or rime and onset, we are being edged away from the democracy that is our birthright. We are being forced to regard the trivial as central, and the central as trivial. When we are sitting a test (or administrating one) we will not be doing anything that might change the world.

Poetry, with the help of dance, drama and music, leads us to the centre of what it is to be. Tunnicliffe (1984) writes: '... poetry can be the holistic element in English teaching'. I think it can be the holistic element in all teaching. Poetry goes to the centre of our language, and, by that token, to the centre of what it is to be a human being.

Bibliography

Ackroyd, P. (1984) *T. S. Eliot*, London: Penguin.

Amis, M. (1986) *The Observer*, 16 February.

Auden, W. H. (1976) *Collected Poems*, Edward Mendelson (ed.), London: Faber and Faber.

Auden, W. H. and Garrett, J. (1935) (eds) *The Poet's Tongue*, London: George Bell.

Barthes, R. (1982) *A Barthes Reader*, Susan Soutag (ed.), London: Cape.

Benet, W. R. (1973) *The Reader's Encyclopaedia*, 2nd edn, London: Book Club Associates.

Benton, M., Teasey, J., Bell, R. and Hurst, K. (1988) *Young Readers Responding to Poems*, London: Routledge.

Brodsky, J. (1987) *Less Than One: Selected Essays*, London: Penguin.

Brownjohn, S. (1980) *Does it Have to Rhyme?: Teaching Children to Write Poetry*, London: Hodder and Stoughton.

Brownjohn, S. (1982) *What Rhymes with Secret?: Teaching Children to Write Poetry*, London: Hodder and Stoughton.

Brownjohn, S. (1989) *The Ability to Name Cats: Teaching Children to Write Poetry*, London: Hodder and Stoughton.

Brownjohn, S. (2002) *The Poet's Craft*, London: Hodder and Stoughton.

Bibliography

Causley, C. (1970) *Figgie Hobbin: Poems for Children*, London: Macmillan.

Clegg, A. B. (ed.) (1965) *The Excitement of Writing*, London: Chatto and Windus.

Corbett, P. and Moses, B. (1986) *Catapults and Kingfishers: Teaching Poetry in Primary Schools*, Oxford: Oxford University Press.

Danby, J. (1940) *Approach to Poetry*, London: Heinemann.

Dixon, P. (1979) *The Silver Toilet Roll*, Winchester: Peter Dixon.

Eliot, T. S. (1963) *Collected Poems*, London: Faber and Faber.

Forster, E. M. (1941) *Howards End*, London: Penguin.

Fowler, H. W. (1996) *The New Fowler's Modern English Usage*, 3rd edn, R. W. Burchfield (ed.), Oxford: Clarendon Press.

Gray, M. (1984) *A Dictionary of Literary Terms*, Harlow: Longman.

Hallworth, G. (1994) *Buy a Penny Ginger and Other Rhymes*, Harlow: Longman.

Heaney, S. (1966) *Death of a Naturalist*, London: Faber.

Heaney, S. (1996) *The Spirit Level*, London: Faber.

Heaney, S. and Hughes, T. (eds) (1982) *The Rattle Bag*, London: Faber.

Hughes, T. (1997) *Tales from Ovid: Twenty-four Passages From the Metamorphoses*, London: Faber.

Joyce, J. (1993) *Ulysses*, J. Johnson (ed.), Oxford: Oxford University Press.

Keegan, P. (ed.) (2000) *The New Penguin Book of English Verse*, London: Penguin.

Langdon, M. (1961) *Let the Children Write: An Explanation of Intensive Writing*, London: Longman.

Larkin, P. (1988) *Collected Poems*, London: Faber.

Longmans Concise English Dictionary (1985), Harlow: Longman.

Merrick, B. (1989) *Talking with Charles Causley*, National Association for the Teaching of English.

Mole, J. (2002) 'Tune, argument, colour, truth', *Signal* 98.

Opie, I. and Opie, P. (1955) *The Oxford Nursery Rhyme Book*, Oxford: Oxford University Press.

Opie, I. and Opie, P. (1959) *The Lore and Language of Schoolchildren*, Oxford: Oxford University Press.

Opie, I. and Opie, P. (1973) *The Oxford Book of Children's Verse*, Oxford: Oxford University Press.

Opie, I. and Opie, P. (1988) *The Singing Game*, Oxford: Oxford University Press.

Richter, I. A. (1980) *The Notebooks of Leonardo da Vinci*, Oxford: Oxford University Press.

Ricks, C. (ed.) (1999) *The Oxford Book of English Verse*, Oxford: Oxford University Press.

Rosen, M. and Steele, S. (1982) *Inky Pinky Ponky: Children's Playground Rhymes*, London: Collins.

Rosenblatt, L. (1978) *The Reader, The Text, The Poem*, Carbondale: Southern Illinois Press.

Sedgwick, F. (1997) *Read My Mind: Young Children, Poetry and Learning*, London: Routledge Falmer.

Sedgwick, F. (1999a) *Shakespeare and the Young Writer*, London: Routledge Falmer.

Sedgwick, F. (1999b) *Thinking About Literacy: Young Children and their Language*, London: Routledge Falmer.

Sedgwick, F. (2000a) *Writing to Learn*, London: Routledge Falmer.

Sedgwick, F. (2000b) *Jenny Kissed Me: An Anthology*

Bibliography

of Poems About Love with Teaching Resources for *Key Stage 2*, Birmingham: Questions.

Sedgwick, F. (2001) *Teaching Literacy: A C[...] Approach*, London: Continuum.

Sedgwick, F. (2002a) *Will There Really Be A Mo[...] Life a Guide. Poems for Key Stage 2 with Te[...] Notes*, London: David Fulton.

Sedgwick, F. (2002b) *Enabling Children's Le[...] Through Drawing*, London: David Fulton.

Sedgwick, F. (2002c) *How to Write Poetry and [...] Published*, London: Continuum.

Shorter Oxford English Dictionary (1973), 3r[...] Oxford: Clarendon Press.

Summerfield, G. (1970) *Junior Voices*, (4 vols), L[...] Penguin.

Thomas, D. (1957) *Collected Poems, 1934[...]* London: Dent.

Thomas, R. S. (1993) *Collected Poems 1945[...]* London: Phoenix.

Trench, R. C. (1908) *On the Study of Words*, L[...] Kegan Paul, Trench, Trubner.

Tunnicliffe, S. (1984) *Poetry Experience: Teach[...] Writing Poetry in Secondary Schools*, L[...] Methuen.